The Federal Research and Development Portfolio

Vital Assets

Federal Investment in Research and Development at the Nation's Universities and Colleges

Donna Fossum
Lawrence S. Painter
Elisa Eiseman
Emile Ettedgui
David M. Adamson

Supported by the
National Science Foundation

RAND
Science and Technology

The research described in this report was conducted by the Science and Technology Policy Institute (operated by RAND from 1992 to November 2003) for the National Science Foundation, under contract ENG-9812731.

Library of Congress Cataloging-in-Publication Data

Vital assets : federal investment in research and development at the nation's universities and colleges / Donna Fossum ... [et al.].
  p. cm.
  "MR-1824."
  ISBN 0-8330-3624-6 (pbk.)
  1. Federal aid to research—United States. 2. Universities and colleges—Research—United States—Finance.
I. Fossum, Donna, 1949–

Q180.U5V57 2004
338.973'06—dc22

2004005269

The RAND Corporation is a nonprofit research organization providing objective analysis and effective solutions that address the challenges facing the public and private sectors around the world. RAND's publications do not necessarily reflect the opinions of its research clients and sponsors.

RAND® is a registered trademark.

Published 2004 by the RAND Corporation
1700 Main Street, P.O. Box 2138, Santa Monica, CA 90407-2138
1200 South Hayes Street, Arlington, VA 22202-5050
201 North Craig Street, Suite 202, Pittsburgh, PA 15213-1516
RAND URL: http://www.rand.org/
To order RAND documents or to obtain additional information, contact
Distribution Services: Telephone: (310) 451-7002;
Fax: (310) 451-6915; Email: order@rand.org

About This Analysis

The federal government's investment in the research and development (R&D) being conducted at the nation's universities and colleges has grown considerably in recent years and represents a pivotal part of the U.S. innovation system—one that advances knowledge of the world and provides critical training to the next generation of scientists and engineers.

The analysis in this report assesses that investment. The analysis drew on the RAND Corporation's RaDiUS (Research and Development in the United States) database and was designed to provide an empirical basis for assessing the federal investment in university-based R&D. It builds on work described in *Discovery and Innovation: Federal Research and Development Activities in the Fifty States, District of Columbia, and Puerto Rico* (Fossum et al., 2000). That earlier work, which also drew on the RaDiUS database, created profiles of federal R&D spending and programs for each state and the two territories. Each profile also provided a brief look at the federal R&D funds going to the state or territory's universities and colleges. Subsequent requests for more detailed information on this topic ultimately led to the current report.

Information on federal R&D funds that are going to the nation's universities and colleges can vary considerably depending on the source of the information and how it was collected. The data presented in this report are drawn from official transactional records of the U.S. government rather than from surveys, so the accounting of which universities and colleges received federal funds for the conduct of R&D—as this term is defined by the federal government—in a single fiscal year is more complete and accurate. The results are presented both by state, including the District of Columbia and Puerto Rico, and by individual university and college. Such data have a variety of potential uses, from gauging the competitive status of specific institutions of higher education to underpinning the planning of regional economic development.

About the Office of Science and Technology Policy

The Office of Science and Technology Policy (OSTP) was created in 1976 to provide the President of the United States with timely policy advice and to coordinate the federal investment in science and technology.

About the Science and Technology Policy Institute

Originally created by Congress in 1991 as the Critical Technologies Institute and re-named in 1998, the Science and Technology Policy Institute (S&TPI) is a federally funded research and development center (FFRDC). It is sponsored by the National Science Foundation and was managed by the RAND Corporation from 1992 through November 30, 2003.

The S&TPI's mission is to help improve public policy by conducting objective, independent research and analysis on policy issues that involve science and technology. To this end, the institute

- Supports the Office of Science and Technology Policy and other Executive Branch agencies, offices, and councils;

- Helps science and technology decisionmakers understand the likely consequences of their decisions and choose among alternative policies; and

- Helps improve understanding in both the public and the private sector of the ways in which science and technology can better serve national objectives.

In carrying out its mission, the S&TPI consults broadly with representatives from private industry, institutions of higher education, and other nonprofit institutions.

Inquiries regarding the S&TPI may be directed to the address below.

Stephen Rattien
Director
RAND Science and Technology
1200 South Hayes Street
Arlington, VA 22202-5050
Tel: 703.413.1100, ext. 5219
Web: www.rand.org/scitech

CONTENTS

BACKGROUND AND PURPOSE

Universities and colleges conduct a substantial portion of America's scientific research. Much of this research is funded by federal research and development (R&D) dollars. Federal R&D funds help universities advance general knowledge, support a range of federal missions, train future scientists and engineers, and enhance economic growth in the communities where they operate. Despite the importance of these activities, decisionmakers face difficulty assessing and monitoring the size of this federal R&D investment and its changing profile over time. This difficulty is rooted in a lack of access to accurate, timely, consistent, and comprehensive information about federal funds going to university and college R&D. As a result, funding allocations and policy decisions are often made without adequate information.

This report is intended to provide an empirical basis for assessing the federal investment in university-based R&D. To do this, RAND compiled a comprehensive list of all the federal R&D funds going to every university and college in the 50 states, the District of Columbia, and Puerto Rico (hereafter referred to collectively as "the states"). The analysis used RAND's RaDiUS (Research and Development in the United States) database of federal R&D funding and activities. This report presents the results of the analysis. Specifically, it provides information on

- State-by-state trends in federal funding of R&D at U.S. universities and colleges from FY 1996 through FY 2002,

- Which federal agencies provided what amounts and types of R&D funds to universities and colleges in FY 2002, and

- What levels of R&D funding individual universities and colleges received in FY 2002.

This report is intended as a reference document for national, regional, state, and university decisionmakers and planners interested in assessing the relative competitiveness of particular university systems and individual campuses in obtaining federal R&D funds. It is also intended to stimulate and enable further analysis and assessment of trends, priorities, and resource allocations involving federally funded R&D.

METHODOLOGY AND APPROACH

The data presented in this report come from the RaDiUS database. RaDiUS systematically tracks all federal R&D funds by tracing them from their most aggregate level in the federal government, at which the R&D activities are planned in general, to their most detailed level, at which the R&D is actually conducted. The most-aggregated data presented are for FY 1996 through FY 2002. The most-detailed data are from FY 2002, since this is the most recent fiscal year for which such data are available. For that year, we also identified all individual R&D awards that went to the 126 accredited medical schools located within the nation's universities and colleges. For additional details on the methodology of this analysis, see Appendix B.

CONCLUSIONS AND IMPLICATIONS

The data show that between FY 1996 and FY 2002, total federal R&D funds going to universities and colleges grew from $12.8 billion to $21.4 billion, for an overall increase of 45.7 percent in constant 1996 dollars. The level of increase in federal R&D funds going to universities and colleges between FY 1996 and FY 2002 was more than double the overall increase in total federal R&D funds during the same period in constant 1996 dollars (i.e., 45.7 percent versus 20.9 percent).

Much of this growth was attributable to sizable increases in R&D funding at the Department of Health and Human Services (HHS), most especially the National Institutes of Health. The main recipients of HHS's funds were nonfederal entities, primarily universities and colleges. By far the most striking finding of this analysis was the discovery that, in FY 2002, 45 percent of all federal R&D funds provided to universities and colleges by HHS and all other federal agencies went directly to medical schools. Because some states do not have medical schools and others have many, this pattern skews the distribution of federal R&D funds among the various states considerably.

Implications for Federal R&D Priorities

The profile of federally funded R&D at universities and colleges that emerges from this analysis raises issues of proportionality. Specifically, in the current funding profile, approximately two-thirds of the federal funds going to universities and colleges for the conduct of R&D is focused on only one field of science—life science—and federal R&D funding is concentrated at only a few research universities. These findings raise questions about whether other critical national needs that have substantial R&D components (such as environment, energy, homeland security, and education) are receiving the investment they require and whether the concentration of dollars at a few institutions is shortchanging science students at institutions that receive little or no federal R&D funding.

Implications for Decisionmaking

This analysis provides information that should help clarify several issues for university and college decisionmakers as well as federal agencies.

First, universities and colleges have lacked long-term, consistent data with which to gauge their success at acquiring R&D funding. In the absence of such data, credible comparisons among institutions cannot be made. This analysis enables all universities and colleges with R&D activity to know where they stand relative to other institutions in their ability to obtain federal R&D funds.

Second, the vehicle used to convey federal R&D funds to universities and colleges (i.e., grant versus contract) is important because it establishes the legal "ground rules" for conducting federally funded R&D. This analysis disproves the persistent stereotype that *all* federal R&D funds are conveyed to universities and colleges via peer-reviewed project grants. As a result, all universities and colleges now have accurate information on the funding mechanisms the federal government has actually used to transmit R&D funds to them, so they can better assess intellectual property issues arising from such R&D.

Third, using the data in this report, federal R&D agencies can now specifically target the universities and colleges in the nation that truly need federal assistance to build their R&D capacity.

ACKNOWLEDGMENTS

The authors wish to thank the many people who encouraged us to expand our summary presentation of information on the federal R&D funding going to higher education institutions that was presented in *Discovery and Innovation: Federal Research and Development Activities in the Fifty States, District of Columbia, and Puerto Rico*. In particular, the authors wish to thank Michael E. Davey, Specialist in Science and Technology in the Resources, Science, and Industry Division of the Congressional Research Services, for his insights and advice throughout the preparation of this report, and his willingness to review the drafts of this report. RAND peer reviewer John Adams has also been of great help with this project, as have their other RAND colleagues: Scott Florence, Aaron Kofner, Lisa Sheldone, Connie S. Moreno, Phyllis Gilmore, Stephen Bloodsworth, and Robin Cole.

Affiliated Research Institute—A nonprofit, independently operated research organization that is very closely affiliated with a particular university or college. These research organizations share research facilities and/or faculty/staff with a university or college. See Table C.23 in Appendix C for a list of affiliated research institutes.

Agency—A department, agency, or instrumentality of the U.S. government (see 31 USC 101). The federal agencies featured in this report include the Department of Defense (DOD), the Department of Health and Human Services (HHS), the Department of Energy (DOE), the Department of Agriculture (USDA), the National Aeronautics and Space Administration (NASA), and the National Science Foundation (NSF), which collectively controlled 95 percent of all federal funds devoted to the conduct of R&D in FY 2002.

Applied Research—Systematic study to gain knowledge or understanding necessary to determine the means of a recognized and specific need (see OMB Circular A-11, Section 84). See *Conduct of Research and Development.*

Award—A contract, grant, cooperative agreement, or other legal instrument a federal agency uses to engage the services of a nongovernmental entity to carry out a governmental responsibility or to achieve some purpose.

Basic Research—Systematic study directed toward fuller knowledge or understanding of the fundamental aspects of phenomena and of observable facts without specific applications toward processes or products in mind (see OMB Circular A-11, Section 84). See *Conduct of Research and Development.*

Baseline—All funds reported to the Office of Management and Budget (OMB) as being spent on activities that meet the OMB definition of what constitutes R&D and which therefore fall within the federal R&D portfolio.

Budget Authority—Authority provided by law to incur (i.e., enter into) financial obligations that will result in immediate or future outlays of federal government funds (see *Budget of the United States Government, Analytical Perspectives, Fiscal Year 2002*; and see OMB Circular A-11, Section 20).

College—A postsecondary school that offers general or liberal arts education, usually leading to an associate, bachelor's, master's, doctor's, or first professional degree. Although this term usually encompasses junior colleges and community colleges, this report does not include junior colleges, community colleges, technical schools, or schools granting only associate degrees (see National Center for Education Statistics, "Digest of Education Statistics, 2002," June 2003). See *University*.

Conduct of Research and Development—Systematic creative work undertaken to increase the stock of knowledge, including knowledge of man, culture, and society, and the use of this stock of knowledge to devise new applications. Includes Basic Research, Applied Research, and Development and the administrative expenses associated with each. Excludes research and development facilities and equipment. Also excludes routine product testing, quality control, mapping, collection of general-purpose statistics, experimental production, routine monitoring and evaluation of an operational program, and the training of scientific and technical personnel (see OMB Circular A-11, Section 84). See *Basic Research, Applied Research, and Development.*

Contract—A legal instrument reflecting a relationship between the U.S. government and a state, local government, or other recipient (1) when the principal purpose of the instrument is to acquire (by purchase, lease, or barter) property or services for the direct benefit or use of the U.S. government or (2) when the agency decides in a specific instance that the use of a procurement contract is appropriate (see 31 USC 6303).

Cooperative Agreement—A legal instrument reflecting a relationship between the U.S. government and a state, local government, or other recipient (1) when the principal purpose of the relationship is to transfer a thing of value to the state, local government, or other recipient to carry out a public purpose of support or stimulation authorized by a law of the United States instead of acquiring (by purchase, lease, or barter) property or services for the direct benefit or use of the U.S. government and (2) when substantial involvement is expected between the executive agency and the state, local government, or other recipient when carrying out the activity contemplated in the agreement (see 31 USC 6305). Does not include cooperative research and development agreements. See *Cooperative Research and Development Agreement.*

Cooperative Research and Development Agreement (CRADA)—Any agreement between one or more federal laboratories and one or more nonfederal parties under which the government, through its laboratories, provides personnel, services, facilities, equipment, intellectual property, or other resources with or without reimbursement (but not funds to nonfederal parties) and the nonfederal parties provide funds, personnel, services, facilities, equipment, intellectual property, or other resources toward the conduct of specified research or development efforts which are consistent with the missions of the laboratory; except that such term does not include a procurement contract or cooperative agreement as those terms are used in sections 6303, 6304, and 6305 of Title 31 (see 15 USC 3710a). NOTE: This report does not provide information on CRADAs, and we provide this definition solely to enable readers to understand the differences between CRADAs and cooperative agreements.

Development—The systematic application of knowledge or understanding, directed toward the production of useful materials, devices, and systems or methods, including design, development, and improvement of prototypes and new processes to meet specific requirements (see OMB Circular A-11, Section 84). See *Conduct of Research and Development.*

Discretionary Spending—Budgetary resources provided in appropriation acts, except those provided to fund mandatory spending programs (i.e., entitlements and food stamps) (see OMB Circular A-11, Section 20).

Enrollment—The total number of students registered in a given school unit at a given time, generally in the fall of a year (see U.S. Department of Education, National Center for Education Statistics, "Digest of Education Statistics, 2002," June 2003).

Experimental Program to Stimulate Competitive Research (EPSCoR)—A program Congress established in 1978 and placed under the auspices of the National Science Foundation (NSF) to assist states that have historically received fewer federal R&D funds. The objective is to increase the ability of academic institutions in these states to compete for such funds and thereby to develop the science and technology resources in the states that support the creation of economic opportunities (i.e., businesses and jobs) for their citizens. To participate in EPSCoR, states must be willing to provide at least partial funding for all approved projects so that the endeavor is a true partnership with the federal government. In 2002, 22 states (Alabama, Alaska, Arkansas, Delaware, Hawaii, Idaho, Kansas, Kentucky, Louisiana, Maine, Mississippi, Montana, Nebraska, Nevada, New Mexico, North Dakota, Oklahoma, South Carolina, South Dakota, Vermont, West Virginia, and Wyoming), the Commonwealth of Puerto Rico, and the U.S. Virgin Islands participated in NSF's EPSCoR program. (Note that the U.S. Virgin Islands was not in the earlier analysis, reported on in *Discovery and Innovation: Federal Research and Development Activities in the Fifty States, District of Columbia, and Puerto Rico*, MR-1194-OSTP/NSF, RAND Corporation, 2000, and therefore is not included in this report.) In 2003, Delaware and Tennessee also joined the program. Also note that, in recent years, other federal agencies (i.e., DOD, DOE, USDA, HHS, NASA, and EPA) have begun similar programs based on the EPSCoR concept.

Expenditure—"A disbursement of funds" (*Merriam Webster's Collegiate Dictionary*, 10th ed., 1993). NSF defines *expenditures* as "funds actually spent by an institution during its fiscal year" (National Science Foundation, Division of Science Resources Statistics, "Academic Research and Development Expenditures: Fiscal Year 2001," Arlington, VA [NSF 03-316], April 2003). See *Outlay.*

Faculty—Members of the instruction and/or research staff who are employed full or part time, as defined by the institution (see U.S. Department of Education, National Center for Education Statistics, "Digest of Education Statistics, 2002," June 2003).

Federally Funded Research and Development Center (FFRDC)—An FFRDC meets some special long-term research or development need that cannot be met as effectively by existing in-house or contractor resources. FFRDCs enable agencies to use private-sector resources to accomplish tasks that are integral to the mission and operation of the sponsoring agency. To discharge its responsibilities to the sponsoring agency, an FFRDC has access, beyond what is common in a normal contractual relationship, to government and supplier data, including sensitive and proprietary data, and to employees and facilities. An FFRDC is required to conduct its business in a manner befitting its special relationship with the government, to operate in the public interest with objectivity and independence, to be free from organizational conflicts of interest, and to have full disclosure of its affairs to the sponsoring agency. It is not the government's intent that an FFRDC use its privileged information or access to facilities to compete with the private sector. However, an FFRDC may perform work other than that for the sponsoring agency under the Economy Act, or other applicable legislation, when the work is not otherwise available from the private sector. Each of the 36 FFRDCs the federal government currently sponsors is administered (i.e., operated) by an industrial firm, university, or nonprofit institution (see Federal Acquisition Regulations [FAR] 35.017).

First Professional Degree Student—A student pursuing an award that requires completion of a program that meets all the following criteria:

- The academic requirements must be completed to begin practice in the profession,

- At least two years of college work must be completed before entering the program, and

- Program completion requires a total of at least six academic years of college work, including both prior required college work and the length of the professional program itself.

First professional degrees may be awarded in the following ten fields: chiropractic (DC or DCM), osteopathic medicine (DO), dentistry (DDS or DMD), pharmacy (PharmD), law (LLB or JD), podiatry (DPM, DP, or PodD), medicine (MD), theology (MDiv, MHL, BD, or Ordination), optometry (OD), and veterinary medicine (DVM) (see U.S. Department of Education, National Center for Education Statistics, Integrated Postsecondary Education Data System [IPEDS], Fall 2000). Does not include graduate students. See *Graduate Student*.

Fiscal Year—The federal government's accounting period. It begins on October 1 and ends on September 30 and is designated by the calendar year in which it ends (see OMB Circular A-11, Section 20).

Formula Grant—Allocation of money to states or their subdivisions according to a formula prescribed by law or administrative regulation, for continuing activities that are not confined to a specific project (see Catalog of Federal Domestic Assistance, GSA, 2002). See *Grant*. Note that, for the purposes of this report, all grants awarded under Catalog of Federal Domestic Assistance (CFDA) Program 10.216 were treated as formula grants instead of project grants because only 18 institutions of higher education in the nation were eligible to receive federal R&D grant funds under this program, and these were the same 18 institutions that received substantially larger formula grants each year under the closely related CFDA Program 10.205.

Graduate Student—A student who holds a bachelor's or first professional degree, or the equivalent, and who is working toward a master's or doctor's degree. Does not include first professional degree students (U.S. Department of Education, National

Center for Education Statistics, "Digest of Education Statistics, 2002," June 2003). See *First Professional Degree Student.*

Grant—A legal instrument reflecting a relationship between the U.S. government and a state, local government, or other recipient (1) when the principal purpose of the relationship is to transfer a thing of value to the state or local government or other recipient to carry out a public purpose of support or stimulation authorized by a law of the United States instead of acquiring (by purchase, lease, or barter) property or services for the direct benefit or use of the U.S. government and (2) when substantial involvement is not expected between the executive agency and the state, local government, or other recipient when carrying out the activity contemplated in the agreement (see 31 USC 6304). See *Project Grant* and *Formula Grant.*

Historically Black College or University (HBCU)—An accredited institution of higher education established prior to 1964 with the principal mission of educating black Americans. The Higher Education Act of 1965, as amended, defines an HBCU as "any historically black college or university that was established prior to 1964, whose principal mission was, and is, the education of black Americans. . . ." Federal regulations (see 20 USC 1061[2]) allow certain exceptions to the founding date (U.S. Department of Education, National Center for Education Statistics, "Digest of Education Statistics, 2002," June 2003).

Land-Grant University (includes 1890 Schools)—Established by the passage of the first Morrill Act of 1862, which facilitated the establishment of colleges through grants of land or of funds in lieu of land. The Morrill Act was intended to provide a broad segment of the population with a practical education that had direct relevance to their daily lives. 1890 Land-Grant Colleges and Universities and Tuskegee University are historically black land-grant colleges and universities (HBCUs) established through the Second Morrill Act of August 30, 1890, which expanded the system of land-grant universities to include historically black institutions in states in which segregation denied minorities access to the land-grant institution established by the First Morrill Act, in 1862. Through the Second Morrill Act and several other authorities, these institutions may receive federal funds for agricultural research, extension, and teaching (see United States Department of Agriculture Cooperative State Research, Education, and Extension Service Acronyms and Commonly Used Terms, 2003).

Medical School (note that this term *excludes* osteopathic, chiropractic, and podiatry schools when used in this report)—An institution offering a program of medical education leading to the MD degree. Virtually all state licensing boards require that U.S. medical schools be accredited by the Liaison Committee on Medical Education (LCME) as a condition for licensing their graduates to practice medicine within a state. Currently, the LCME accredits 126 programs at universities and colleges within the United States, all of which lead to the MD degree (see Liaison Committee on Medical Education, Directory of Accredited Medical Education Programs, available at http://www.lcme.org/directry.htm as of March 3, 2004). Note that the term *medical school*, as used in this report, does *not* encompass hospitals or medical centers (i.e., so-called "teaching" hospitals) that are in some way "affiliated with" or "connected to" a university or college and/or its "medical school." Instead, the term refers *only* to the 126 programs within universities and colleges that provide medical education leading to the MD degree.

Obligations—Binding agreements that will result in outlays (see *Outlay*) immediately or in the future. That is, the amounts of orders placed, contracts awarded, services received, and similar transactions during a given period that will require payments during the same or a future period. Budgetary resources must be available before obligations can be incurred legally (see Budget of the United States Government, Analytical Perspectives, Fiscal Years 2002; OMB Circular A-11, Section 20).

Outlay—A payment to liquidate an obligation (other than the repayment of debt principal). Outlays are generally equal to cash disbursements, and they are the measure of government spending (see Budget of the United States Government, Analytical Perspectives, Fiscal Years 2002; OMB Circular A-11, Section 20). See *Expenditure.*

Private University or College—A university or college that is controlled by an individual or agency other than a state, a subdivision of a state, or the federal government and that is usually supported primarily by other than public funds, and the operation of whose program rests with other than publicly elected or appointed officials. Private schools and institutions include both nonprofit and proprietary institutions (see U.S. Department of Education, National Center for Education Statistics, "Digest of Education Statistics, 2002," June 2003).

Project Grant—The funding, for fixed or known periods, of specific projects for the delivery of specific services or products without liability for damages for failure to perform (see Catalog of Federal Domestic Assistance, GSA, 2002). See *Grant.*

Public University or College—A university or college controlled and operated by publicly elected or appointed officials and deriving its primary support from public funds (see U.S. Department of Education, National Center for Education Statistics, "Digest of Education Statistics, 2002," June 2003).

Research and Development (R&D)—Throughout this report, this term refers *only* to the *Conduct of Research and Development,* as defined above.

Research and Development Equipment—The acquisition or design and production of major equipment for R&D. Includes expendable or movable equipment (e.g., spectrometers, research satellites, and detectors). Excludes routine purchases of ordinary office equipment or furniture and fixtures. (See OMB Circular A-11, Section 84.)

Research and Development Facilities—The construction and rehabilitation of R&D facilities. Includes the acquisition, design, and construction of, or major repairs or alterations to, all physical facilities for use in R&D activities. Facilities include land, buildings, and fixed capital equipment, regardless of whether the facilities are to be used by the government or by a private organization and regardless of where title to the property may rest. The term also includes the International Space Station and such fixed facilities as reactors, wind tunnels, and particle reactors, but excludes movable R&D equipment. (See OMB Circular A-11, Section 84.)

Science and Engineering—The disciplines in the fields of Engineering, Physical Sciences, Mathematical Sciences, Computer Sciences, Life Sciences, Psychology, and Social Sciences (see National Science Foundation, Division of Science Resources Statistics, "Survey of Graduate Students and Postdoctorates in Science and Engineering: Fall 2000 [Methodology Report]," Arlington, VA , July 2002).

Undergraduate Student—A student registered at an institution of higher education who is working in a program leading to a baccalaureate degree or other formal award below the baccalaureate, such as an associate degree (see U.S. Department of Education, National Center for Education Statistics, "Digest of Education Statistics, 2002," June 2003).

University—An institution of higher education consisting of a liberal arts college, a diverse graduate program, and usually two or more professional schools or faculties and empowered to confer degrees in various fields of study (see U.S. Department of Education, National Center for Education Statistics, "Digest of Education Statistics, 2002," June 2003). See *College.*

Chapter One

INTRODUCTION

BACKGROUND

Innovation based on scientific and technological progress makes major contributions to U.S. economic prosperity, national security, and other national goals. The system that supports such innovation consists of a complex network of institutions that conduct research and development (R&D) in a range of settings, including universities, industry, and government. Because of the success of this system, it has been accurately characterized as a vital national asset.[1] A hallmark of the U.S. innovation system, as distinct from such systems in other industrialized nations, is its heavy reliance on universities and colleges to conduct federally funded R&D. In Japan and Europe, for instance, specialized research institutes and government-operated laboratories carry out a much higher fraction of federal R&D than such institutions do in the United States,[2] where universities and colleges perform between 20 and 25 percent of it. Since World War II, a steady infusion of federal R&D funds has helped transform many U.S. universities into research-focused institutions. Indeed, in FY 2002, federal funds were paying for R&D being conducted at almost 800 of the nation's more than 1,825 university and college campuses.

Federal R&D funds contribute substantially to three important university functions. First, they enable universities and colleges to sustain R&D programs in scientific and engineering fields that might otherwise have difficulty securing financial support. This R&D expands the collective knowledge of the world and, at the same time, helps fulfill the basic missions of a number of federal agencies. Before World War II, the major sources of funding for university R&D were state governments, industry, and foundations. The federal entry into the funding of university R&D represented an admission that these sources were not stable enough to grow and sustain this vital component of the U.S. innovation system. In particular, it showed that the federal government, unlike industry, was willing to support the conduct of long-term, high-risk basic research at the nation's universities and colleges.

Second, federally funded R&D supports the education and training of graduate students in scientific and engineering fields, typically through research assistantships. Thus, universities and colleges not only expand the knowledge base, they also edu-

---

[1] Popper and Wagner, 2002, p. ix.
[2] Mowery and Rosenberg, 1993, p. 48.

1

cate the next generation of scientists and engineers, whose expertise will drive technological innovation.

Third, the federally funded R&D that universities and colleges perform contributes significantly to the economic benefits that can accrue to the cities, states, and regions in which the institutions are located. Universities that have medical schools—which the federal government supports heavily in nearly every case—are often the major employers in the cities where they are located. Such is the case in Ann Arbor, Baltimore, Cambridge, Madison, New Haven, and Vermilion. And universities and colleges that do not have medical schools are also the major employers in their home cities in many instances. Such is indeed the case in Ames, Boise, Boulder, College Station, Eugene, Knoxville, Lincoln, Princeton, and Provo, where the local universities and colleges—which, regardless of not having medical schools, still have sizable research communities funded in part by federal dollars—are the largest employers of the local population. Universities and colleges thus may constitute a major part of a city's or region's economic base.

Given the importance of federal R&D funds for advancing general knowledge, fulfilling federal missions, training future scientists and engineers, and ensuring the prosperity of universities and colleges and the economic settings in which they operate, it is important to assess and monitor the size and profile of the federal investment in this area. Although RAND conducted a preliminary study of this topic,[3] federal policymakers, states, and the higher education community have still lacked the data to perform the needed analyses. In particular, they have lacked access to accurate, timely, consistent, and comprehensive spending information for federally funded university and college R&D.[4]

As the National Science Board (NSB) noted in 2001, "Available data and analyses are often ill-suited for informing budget allocation decisions that affect the U.S. research infrastructure."[5] Among the data problems the NSB report cited were a lack of timeliness and inconsistent definitions:

> Data on federal research funding, especially at the field level, are often unavailable on a timely basis to inform budget allocation decisions, use outdated research field definitions, fail to capture important characteristics of research activities—particularly growing collaboration across fields, organizations, sectors, and even nations—and suffer from inconsistent applications of definitions across reporting units.[6]

Often, existing data on expenditures are collected via surveys, which may lump R&D spending in with other types of federal assistance (such as facilities or overhead reimbursements) and whose results may also be several years out of date by the time they are publicly released. Moreover, the inconsistent application of definitions,

---

[3] Fossum et al., 2000.

[4] Popper and Wagner (2002, p. 48) note that analysts' understanding of the U.S. innovation system has grown increasingly sophisticated in the past decade but has been hampered by weak or nonexistent data along many dimensions, including expenditures.

[5] National Science Board, 2001, p. 2.

[6] National Science Board, 2001, p. 19.

which is particularly apparent in the surveys of federal R&D funding of institutions of higher education, frustrates the planning efforts of universities and colleges and of governments.[7]

PURPOSE OF THIS REPORT

This report describes our effort to address these data issues through an analysis designed to provide a more solid foundation for assessing the federal investment in university-based R&D. As the basis for our analysis, we compiled a comprehensive list of all federally funded R&D activities at every university and college in the 50 states, the District of Columbia, and Puerto Rico (hereafter referred to collectively as "the states") by drawing on RAND's RaDiUS (Research and Development in the United States) database of federal R&D funding and activities. This report presents the results of this analysis, including data on

- State-by-state trends in the federal funding of R&D at the nation's universities and colleges from FY 1996 through FY 2002,

- Which federal agencies provided what amounts and types of R&D funds to universities and colleges in FY 2002, and

- What levels of R&D funding individual universities and colleges received in FY 2002.

This report is intended to be a reference document for national, regional, state, and university decisionmakers and planners interested in assessing the relative competitiveness of particular university systems and individual campuses in obtaining federal R&D funds. It is also intended to be both a stimulus and a tool for further analysis and assessment of trends, priorities, and resource allocations in federally funded R&D.

METHODOLOGY AND APPROACH

All data presented in this report are from the RaDiUS database. RaDiUS systematically tracks all federal funds spent each year on the "conduct of R&D" by tracing them from their most aggregated level in the federal government to the performer level—i.e., the level at which the R&D is actually conducted. Neither the RaDiUS database nor this report contains any information on federal funds spent for the construction or rehabilitation of R&D facilities or for the design, production, and/or purchase of R&D equipment. Note that all references to federal R&D funds in this report denote *only* the federal dollars spent on the "conduct of R&D."

Note also that the term *R&D* may not encompass some activities supported with federal funds that reasonable people might consider to be "research," solely because the federal funds spent on these activities were not designated by an official of the federal government as being "R&D" dollars. In other words, a federal procurement

---

[7] Davey and Rowberg, 2000, p. 14.

official determined that a specific federally funded project was an "assessment of a complex issue in support of policy development and decision making" (non-R&D) rather than a "systematic study of some topic that will increase scientific knowledge" (R&D). Consequently, the official formally categorized that project as "study and analysis" rather than as "R&D." This difference in how a project is designated means that RaDiUS tracks federal dollars spent on projects designated as "R&D" but does not track those spent on projects designated as "study and analysis." And, finally, note that the term *R&D*, as used by the federal government, is not synonymous with *science and technology (S&T)*. For additional information on the terms *R&D* and *S&T*, as well as on RaDiUS and the data that RaDiUS does and does not include, see Appendix A.

The most-aggregated data we present in this report are for FY 1996 through FY 2002; the most-detailed data are from FY 2002 only, which is the most recent fiscal year for which this information is available. To facilitate much of the analysis that is central to this report, we identified all the individual R&D awards that went to the 126 accredited medical schools located within the nation's universities and colleges. We also excluded federal funds going to universities for the management and operation of federally funded R&D centers (FFRDCs). While we would have preferred to distinguish between federal R&D awards going to universities and colleges that were and were not congressionally earmarked, such a distinction was not possible. As a result, we did not separately analyze the portion of federal R&D funds that were congressionally earmarked in FY 2002 that went to universities and colleges for the conduct of R&D, which is estimated to be between 6 and 7 percent of the total R&D funds going to universities and colleges (see Appendix B). Instead, these funds are mixed in with the grants that were awarded based on merit or formulas.

All funding amounts that we present for states and individual universities and colleges are "obligations." They show the total dollars that the federal government has agreed in a specific fiscal year to provide to a university or college to cover the costs of R&D work that will be performed by the university or college in that fiscal year *or* in some future fiscal year. The federal government records all of its transactions that result in monetary awards to third parties (e.g., universities and colleges) only as "obligations"; hence, this was the only unit of measure available for our analysis. Please note that "obligation*s*" are not the same as "outlays" or "expenditures," the latter of which involve the disbursement of funds for use in the current fiscal year only, as opposed to some future fiscal year as well. This distinction is important, because an obligation of funds by the federal government to a university or college for an unusually long-term or extraordinarily large R&D project can have a notable effect on the total amount of federal R&D funds credited to a single institution in a given fiscal year. Such awards are not common, however, so the amount of federal R&D funds going to specific universities and colleges customarily trends more evenly from one fiscal year to the next. In FY 2002, however, the Applied Physics Laboratory at Johns Hopkins University received incremental funding on two such uncommon federal R&D awards, which together totaled $330 million. While these two awards had a noticeable effect on the total dollars Johns Hopkins received, they did not affect its number-one ranking among the nation's universities and colleges that received federal R&D funds. These two awards were so large, however, that they affected the overall state ranking of Maryland, the home of Johns Hopkins, when all federal R&D funds going to the universities and colleges resident in each state were totaled. Specifically, Maryland rose from sixth place among the states in FY 2001 to fourth place in FY 2002, "leapfrogging" over both Texas and Massachusetts (see Tables 2.1 and 2.2 in Chapter 2). Had Johns Hopkins not received the incremental funding on these two awards in FY 2002, Maryland would have kept its FY 2001 ranking, remaining sixth among the states in FY 2002.

Appendix B provides additional details on the methodology of our analysis.

HOW THIS REPORT IS ORGANIZED

Chapter Two presents an overview of our findings, drawn from the tables of four-year accredited U.S. universities and colleges in Appendix D. These tables, one for each state, show the amount of federal R&D funds that each university and college received from the federal government in FY 2002, data drawn from the RaDiUS database. (The tables are presented on a CD-ROM attached to the back cover of this report.) Appendix D also provides the size of each college and university's student body and faculty, as well as the federal R&D funds per capita that each institution received. Information on the degrees each institution awards and whether the institution is public, private, land grant, and/or historically black is also given. Descriptions of the sources for all the data in the tables are provided at the very beginning of the appendix. Information for FY 1996 through FY 2001 is based on data extracted directly from the RaDiUS database.

Chapter Three presents our main conclusions and explores the implications of this analysis for future discussions. Following Chapter Three are four appendices that add detail to the analysis and findings discussed throughout the text. Appendix A describes the RaDiUS database; Appendix B discusses in detail the methodology we used in the analysis. Appendix C presents a number of tables containing additional details on the universities and colleges that received the most federal R&D funds in FY 2002 (the tables are presented on the attached CD-ROM). And, as noted above, Appendix D details the federal R&D funds that every four-year accredited university and college in the nation received in FY 2002.

Chapter Two

FEDERAL R&D FUNDS TO UNIVERSITIES AND COLLEGES

OVERALL TRENDS

In recent years, the annual funding that the federal government provides to universities and colleges for R&D has grown disproportionately compared with the growth in both total federal discretionary and total federal R&D funding. Specifically, in the seven-year period from FY 1996 through FY 2002:

- Total federal discretionary funds grew from $501.0 billion to $734.7 billion, for an increase of 46.7 percent in current dollars and an increase of 27.9 percent in constant 1996 dollars (President's Budget 2004).

- Total federal R&D funds grew from $69.7 billion to $96.6 billion, for an increase of 38.6 percent in current dollars and an increase of 20.9 percent in constant 1996 dollars (RaDiUS).

- Total federal R&D funds going to universities and colleges grew from $12.8 billion to $21.4 billion, after a slight dip in FY 1997, for an overall increase of 67.2 percent in current dollars and an overall increase of 45.7 percent in constant 1996 dollars (RaDiUS).

In short, between FY 1996 and FY 2002, the average annual increase in "total federal R&D funds" was only 5.7 percent in current dollars and 3.3 percent in constant 1996 dollars, while the average annual increase in the "federal R&D funds going to universities and colleges" was 9.0 percent in current dollars and 6.6 percent in constant 1996 dollars, indicating that, in recent years, an ever greater share of federal R&D funds has been going to the nation's universities and colleges.

As Figures 2.1 and 2.2 show, between FY 1996 and FY 2002, the R&D funds grew for all but one major federal R&D agency, the National Aeronautics and Space Administration (NASA). In FY 2000, NASA decided to change the budgetary status of the Space Station program, thereby removing the funds for that program from the "conduct of R&D" category and thus causing NASA's R&D total to drop. The agency whose R&D funding levels increased the most was the Department of Health and Human Services (HHS), the home of the National Institutes of Health. Between FY 1996 and FY 2002, the R&D funds controlled by HHS more than doubled, which has led to HHS now controlling almost 25 percent of all federal dollars devoted to the conduct of R&D. Since HHS awards around 90 percent of these R&D funds to extramural (i.e.,

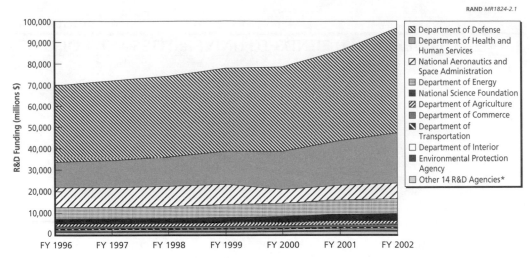

RAND *MR1824-2.1*

*Altogether, these agencies received less than $400M in each fiscal year between 1996 and 2002.

Figure 2.1—Total Funding in Current Dollars for Conduct of R&D in FY 1996–2002, by Federal Agency (Budget Authority in Millions)

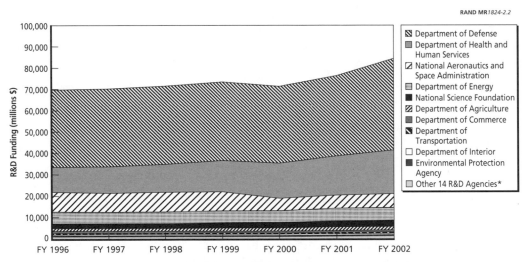

RAND **MR***1824-2.2*

*Altogether, these agencies received less than $400M in each fiscal year between 1996 and 2002.

Figure 2.2—Total Funding in Constant 1996 Dollars for Conduct of R&D in FY 1996–2002, by Federal Agency (Budget Authority in Millions)

nonfederal) performers each year and gives nearly 75 percent of all of its extramural R&D funds to the nation's universities and colleges annually, this increase has had a major influence on the amount of R&D funds available to U.S. universities and colleges. Many other federal agencies also provide R&D funds to the nation's universities and colleges, but HHS has been the driving force in this area for the past several years.

Tables 2.1 and 2.2 show that, between FY 1996 and FY 2002,

- The total federal R&D funds going to universities and colleges increased by 67 percent in current dollars and 46 percent in constant 1996 dollars.

- At least one university or college in every state received federal R&D funds.

- The relative ranking of the states according to how much federal R&D funding their resident universities and colleges received changed little, with almost 80 percent shifting no more than two places in the overall rankings between these years.

- In each fiscal year, over 55 percent of all federal R&D funds awarded to the nation's universities and colleges went to institutions in only nine states: California, Illinois, Maryland, Massachusetts, Michigan, New York, North Carolina, Pennsylvania, and Texas. These were the only states to rank in the top ten in all seven fiscal years.

Table 2.1

Federal Funds in Current Dollars Provided to Universities and Colleges, Including Medical Schools, for Conduct of R&D in FY 1996–2002, by State in Rank Order (Obligations in Millions)

	FY 1996		FY 1997		FY 1998		FY 1999		FY 2000		FY 2001		FY 2002	
Total	12,773		12,667		14,456		15,890		17,537		19,115		21,352	
Rank														
1	CA	1,754	CA	1,747	CA	2,011	CA	2,108	CA	2,371	CA	2,505	CA	2,726
2	NY	1,059	NY	1,093	NY	1,213	NY	1,326	NY	1,451	NY	1,562	NY	1,670
3	MA	873	MA	834	MD	979	MA	1,108	MA	1,130	PA	1,163	PA	1,327
4	MD	791	PA	767	MA	938	MD	1,054	MD	1,101	TX	1,130	MD	1,303
5	PA	754	MD	725	PA	904	PA	1,006	PA	1,094	MA	1,096	TX	1,256
6	TX	698	TX	685	TX	775	TX	867	TX	959	MD	1,034	MA	1,196
7	IL	542	NC	501	NC	560	IL	642	IL	664	IL	760	NC	858
8	NC	501	IL	492	IL	555	NC	566	NC	652	NC	744	IL	818
9	MI	417	MI	423	MI	469	MI	507	MI	551	MI	611	MI	659
10	WA	359	WA	362	WA	391	WA	437	OH	466	WA	543	OH	588
11	OH	336	OH	336	OH	367	MO	417	WA	466	OH	525	WA	577
12	MN	273	MN	282	FL	332	OH	407	FL	425	FL	448	MO	519
13	GA	263	CO	278	CO	318	FL	335	MO	403	MO	445	FL	491
14	WI	261	GA	271	GA	316	CO	335	GA	384	GA	420	GA	489
15	MO	260	FL	268	MO	308	GA	325	CO	369	WI	410	WI	468
16	CO	259	MO	268	MN	296	MN	320	WI	368	MN	409	MN	465
17	CT	255	CT	262	WI	281	CT	318	MN	360	CO	408	CO	434
18	FL	254	WI	253	CT	277	WI	317	CT	346	CT	367	CT	414
19	AL	240	AL	244	AL	271	AL	269	AL	306	VA	356	AL	388
20	NJ	205	VA	207	VA	234	VA	262	VA	292	AL	347	VA	386
21	VA	204	NJ	203	NJ	228	NJ	233	NJ	285	TN	288	TN	383
22	IN	198	IN	199	IN	201	IN	216	IN	254	OR	279	NJ	314
23	OR	157	OR	170	OR	183	OR	216	OR	231	NJ	271	OR	288
24	AZ	157	TN	154	AZ	175	AZ	199	AZ	220	IN	262	IN	285
25	TN	146	AZ	146	IA	164	TN	186	TN	218	IA	224	AZ	250
26	DC	142	IA	139	TN	157	IA	172	IA	179	AZ	218	IA	246
27	IA	141	DC	131	UT	151	UT	161	UT	167	DC	194	DC	216
28	LA	134	UT	130	DC	135	DC	154	DC	155	UT	189	UT	215
29	UT	130	LA	120	LA	129	LA	142	LA	147	LA	162	LA	180
30	NM	95	SC	90	SC	111	SC	109	SC	123	SC	146	SC	167

Table 2.1 (continued)

Rank	FY 1996		FY 1997		FY 1998		FY 1999		FY 2000		FY 2001		FY 2002	
31	SC	80	NM	82	NM	91	NM	103	KY	114	NM	140	KY	150
32	KY	73	RI	71	KS	85	KY	91	NH	109	KY	134	NH	138
33	NH	70	KY	67	KY	75	KS	91	NM	104	KS	131	HI	134
34	RI	70	NH	64	NH	71	NH	88	KS	101	NH	119	NM	133
35	HI	62	KS	63	MS	69	MS	83	MS	96	HI	109	MS	125
36	KS	61	HI	61	OK	69	RI	79	RI	95	MS	105	KS	119
37	OK	51	OK	54	RI	65	HI	77	HI	86	OK	87	OK	119
38	MS	50	MS	49	HI	64	OK	68	OK	81	RI	87	RI	104
39	WV	45	WV	41	PR	48	PR	53	NE	68	NE	82	NE	99
40	NE	44	NE	40	NE	48	NE	53	PR	64	VT	70	PR	89
41	AR	38	PR	39	WV	44	AR	49	AR	62	AR	66	VT	74
42	PR	38	AR	38	AR	43	VT	47	VT	60	AK	64	WV	71
43	NV	38	VT	35	VT	41	MT	44	DE	52	MT	63	AR	69
44	VT	36	NV	35	NV	39	AK	42	NV	49	PR	63	NV	60
45	DE	33	DE	29	DE	35	DE	40	AK	49	NV	57	AK	58
46	ND	31	AK	27	MT	33	WV	38	WV	46	WV	57	MT	56
47	MT	26	MT	26	AK	28	NV	36	MT	44	DE	45	DE	48
48	AK	23	ND	19	ND	25	ND	30	ND	33	ND	33	ND	41
49	WY	17	ID	14	ME	18	ME	20	ID	26	ID	28	ID	34
50	ID	12	ME	14	WY	17	ID	17	WY	21	ME	24	ME	20
51	ME	10	WY	11	ID	14	WY	15	SD	20	WY	19	WY	18
52	SD	8	SD	9	SD	10	SD	10	ME	20	SD	17	SD	17

NOTE: See Table C.1 in Appendix C for more detailed information.

Table 2.2

Federal Funds in Constant 1996 Dollars Provided to Universities and Colleges, Including Medical Schools, for Conduct of R&D in FY 1996–2002, by State in Rank Order (Obligations in Millions)

Rank	FY 1996		FY 1997		FY 1998		FY 1999		FY 2000		FY 2001		FY 2002	
Total	12,773		12,388		13,922		14,936		15,976		16,936		18,616	
1	CA	1,754	CA	1,708	CA	1,937	CA	1,982	CA	2,160	CA	2,219	CA	2,377
2	NY	1,059	NY	1,069	NY	1,168	NY	1,246	NY	1,322	NY	1,384	NY	1,456
3	MA	873	MA	816	MD	943	MA	1,042	MA	1,029	PA	1,030	PA	1,157
4	MD	791	PA	751	MA	904	MD	990	MD	1,003	TX	1,001	MD	1,136
5	PA	754	MD	709	PA	871	PA	946	PA	997	MA	971	TX	1,095
6	TX	698	TX	670	TX	746	TX	815	TX	874	MD	916	MA	1,043
7	IL	542	NC	490	NC	540	IL	603	IL	605	IL	674	NC	748
8	NC	501	IL	481	IL	534	NC	532	NC	594	NC	659	IL	713
9	MI	417	MI	413	MI	451	MI	477	MI	502	MI	542	MI	574
10	WA	359	WA	354	WA	376	WA	411	OH	425	WA	481	OH	512
11	OH	336	OH	328	OH	353	MO	392	WA	424	OH	465	WA	503
12	MN	273	MN	276	FL	320	OH	383	FL	387	FL	397	MO	453
13	GA	263	CO	272	CO	306	FL	315	MO	367	MO	394	FL	428
14	WI	261	GA	265	GA	305	CO	315	GA	350	GA	372	GA	426
15	MO	260	FL	262	MO	296	GA	306	CO	336	WI	363	WI	408
16	CO	259	MO	262	MN	285	MN	301	WI	335	MN	362	MN	405
17	CT	255	CT	256	WI	271	CT	299	MN	328	CO	361	CO	378
18	FL	254	WI	248	CT	267	WI	298	CT	315	CT	325	CT	361
19	AL	240	AL	238	AL	261	AL	253	AL	279	VA	316	AL	338
20	NJ	205	VA	202	VA	225	VA	247	VA	266	AL	307	VA	337
21	VA	204	NJ	199	NJ	219	NJ	219	NJ	260	TN	255	TN	334
22	IN	198	IN	194	IN	194	IN	203	IN	231	OR	248	NJ	274

Table 2.2 (continued)

Rank	FY 1996		FY 1997		FY 1998		FY 1999		FY 2000		FY 2001		FY 2002	
23	OR	157	OR	166	OR	176	OR	203	OR	211	NJ	240	OR	251
24	AZ	157	TN	151	AZ	169	AZ	187	AZ	200	IN	232	IN	249
25	TN	146	AZ	143	IA	158	TN	175	TN	199	IA	199	AZ	218
26	DC	142	IA	136	TN	151	IA	162	IA	163	AZ	193	IA	215
27	IA	141	DC	128	UT	145	UT	152	UT	152	DC	172	DC	189
28	LA	134	UT	127	DC	130	DC	145	DC	141	UT	168	UT	188
29	UT	130	LA	118	LA	124	LA	134	LA	134	LA	143	LA	157
30	NM	95	SC	88	SC	107	SC	102	SC	112	SC	129	SC	146
31	SC	80	NM	80	NM	87	NM	97	KY	104	NM	124	KY	131
32	KY	73	RI	69	KS	82	KY	85	NH	99	KY	119	NH	120
33	NH	70	KY	65	KY	72	KS	85	NM	95	KS	116	HI	117
34	RI	70	NH	63	NH	68	NH	83	KS	92	NH	105	NM	116
35	HI	62	KS	62	MS	66	MS	78	MS	87	HI	97	MS	109
36	KS	61	HI	60	OK	66	RI	74	RI	86	MS	93	KS	104
37	OK	51	OK	53	RI	63	HI	72	HI	79	OK	77	OK	103
38	MS	50	MS	48	HI	62	OK	64	OK	74	RI	77	RI	91
39	WV	45	WV	40	PR	46	PR	50	NE	62	NE	72	NE	86
40	NE	44	NE	39	NE	46	NE	50	PR	58	VT	62	PR	77
41	AR	38	PR	38	WV	43	AR	46	AR	56	AR	58	VT	65
42	PR	38	AR	37	AR	41	VT	44	VT	55	AK	57	WV	62
43	NV	38	VT	35	VT	39	MT	41	DE	47	MT	56	AR	60
44	VT	36	NV	35	NV	37	AK	39	NV	45	PR	56	NV	53
45	DE	33	DE	28	DE	34	DE	38	AK	44	NV	50	AK	50
46	ND	31	AK	26	MT	32	WV	36	WV	42	WV	50	MT	49
47	MT	26	MT	26	AK	27	NV	34	MT	40	DE	40	DE	42
48	AK	23	ND	19	ND	24	ND	28	ND	30	ND	29	ND	35
49	WY	17	ID	14	ME	17	ME	19	ID	24	ID	25	ID	30
50	ID	12	ME	13	WY	17	ID	16	WY	19	ME	22	ME	18
51	ME	10	WY	10	ID	13	WY	14	SD	18	WY	17	WY	16
52	SD	8	SD	9	SD	10	SD	9	ME	18	SD	15	SD	15

NOTE: See Table C.1 in Appendix C for more detailed information.

The two states in the top ranks whose overall position shifted the most from year to year between FY 1996 and FY 2002—Maryland and Massachusetts—are home to the three largest nonprofit research institutes in the nation that are closely affiliated with a university or college. (See Table C.23 in Appendix C for a complete list of affiliated research institutes.) Specifically, Johns Hopkins University, in Maryland, is home to the Applied Physics Laboratory, which received 33 percent of all federal R&D funds awarded to the university in FY 2001 and 42 percent in FY 2002. The Massachusetts Institute of Technology is home to the Whitehead Institute for Biomedical Research and the Woods Hole Oceanographic Institute (MIT/WHOI Joint Program), which collectively received 37 percent of all federal R&D funds awarded to the university in FY 2001 and 34 percent in FY 2002.

As noted previously, because the amount of federal R&D funds these affiliated research institutes receive tends to vary somewhat from year to year, a single R&D award from a federal agency to one of them can greatly affect the overall ranking of its host state. Such was indeed the case for Maryland in FY 2002, when the Applied Physics Laboratory received incremental funding on a pair of federal R&D contracts that totaled $330 million, which raised Maryland from sixth place among the states in FY 2001 to fourth place in FY 2002. Note, however, that the federal R&D funds these affiliated research institutes received had little, if any, effect on the rankings of their host institutions within a state, because each of them was part of the university that ranked number one, by a large margin, in its respective state. See Appendix D for details on the federal R&D funds going to Johns Hopkins University, the Massachusetts Institute of Technology, and the other institutions of higher education in Maryland and Massachusetts in FY 2002.

THE ROLE OF MEDICAL SCHOOLS

The most significant finding of this analysis is that, of all federal R&D funds that went to the nation's universities and colleges, 42 percent in FY 2001 and 45 percent in FY 2002 went directly to medical schools—academic units present at only a small fraction of the nation's many hundreds of universities and colleges. In light of this discovery, it is not surprising to find that the top ten states in the overall rankings in FY 2002 (see Tables 2.1 and 2.2) are home to 48 percent of the nation's medical schools, and the top 20 states are home to 86 percent of the nation's medical schools. In short, the presence of one or more medical schools at the universities and colleges in a state profoundly affects the amount of federal R&D funds that state's resident universities and colleges receive.

Because some states have *no* medical schools and others have *many*, one way of examining the success of a state's universities and colleges in obtaining federal R&D funds is to exclude the federal R&D funds going to medical schools. This provides a more balanced view of the relative rankings among the states for areas of R&D outside the scope of the medical-based life sciences.

Table 2.3 shows how the states rank in terms of federal R&D funds their universities and colleges received in FY 2002 when the funding that went to medical schools is included and excluded. One set of columns shows the state rankings when the medical school data were included in the analysis, and one set shows the rankings when they were not included. The column on the far right shows how removing the federal R&D dollars going to medical schools affected the rankings. For most states, the removal improved their overall ranking a bit. For 16 states, however, it decreased their overall ranking, indicating that their in-state university-based, federally supported R&D enterprises were dominated by the R&D conducted at their institutions' medical schools. This is particularly the case for the states of Connecticut, Missouri, and Vermont, all of which dropped at least nine places in the rankings when the funds going to medical schools were eliminated.

HOW R&D SUPPORT VARIES BY FEDERAL AGENCY

Twenty-four separate agencies fund all of the federal government's R&D activities. However, 96 percent of federal R&D funds going to the nation's colleges and universities come from only six of these agencies.

Table 2.3

States Ranked According to Total Federal Funds Received for Conduct of R&D in FY 2002 by Their Resident Universities and Colleges, Including and Excluding Medical Schools
(Obligations in Millions)

Including Medical Schools			Excluding Medical Schools			Change in Rank of State
Total		21,352	Total		11,741	
Rank	State	Amount	Rank	State	Amount	
1	California	2,726	1	California	1,578	0
2	New York	1,670	2	Maryland	843	2
3	Pennsylvania	1,327	3	Massachusetts	826	3
4	Maryland	1,303	4	New York	719	-2
5	Texas	1,256	5	Pennsylvania	603	-2
6	Massachusetts	1,196	6	Texas	572	-1
7	North Carolina	858	7	Illinois	452	1
8	Illinois	818	8	Michigan	382	1
9	Michigan	659	9	North Carolina	336	-2
10	Ohio	588	10	Washington	326	1
11	Washington	577	11	Florida	321	2
12	Missouri	519	12	Georgia	292	2
13	Florida	491	13	Wisconsin	276	2
14	Georgia	489	14	Colorado	275	3
15	Wisconsin	468	15	Ohio	273	-5
16	Minnesota	465	16	Alabama[a]	217	3
17	Colorado	434	17	Virginia	214	3
18	Connecticut	414	18	New Jersey	210	4
19	Alabama[a]	388	19	Minnesota	198	-3
20	Virginia	386	20	Indiana	197	4
21	Tennessee	383	21	Arizona	185	4
22	New Jersey	314	22	Oregon	169	1
23	Oregon	288	23	Missouri	163	-11
24	Indiana	285	24	Tennessee	149	-3
			25	District of Columbia	135	2
25	Arizona	250				
26	Iowa	246	26	Iowa	126	0
27	District of Columbia	216	27	Louisiana[a]	124	2
28	Utah	215	28	Hawaii	124	5
29	Louisiana[a]	180	29	Utah	121	-1
30	South Carolina[a]	167	30	Connecticut	115	-12
31	Kentucky[a]	150	31	Mississippi[a]	111	4
32	New Hampshire	138	32	New Mexico[a]	99	2
33	Hawaii	134	33	Oklahoma[a]	86	4
34	New Mexico[a]	133	34	Kansas[a]	83	2
35	Mississippi[a]	125	35	South Carolina[a]	79	-5
36	Kansas[a]	119	36	New Hampshire	77	-4
37	Oklahoma[a]	119	37	Rhode Island	69	1
38	Rhode Island	104	38	Kentucky[a]	68	-7
39	Nebraska[a]	99	39	Nebraska[a]	67	0
40	Puerto Rico[a]	89	40	West Virginia[a]	58	2
41	Vermont[a]	74	41	Alaska[a]	58	4
42	West Virginia[a]	71	42	Montana[a]	56	4
43	Arkansas[a]	69	43	Nevada	49	1
44	Nevada	60	44	Puerto Rico[a]	48	-4
45	Alaska[a]	58	45	Delaware	48	2

Table 2.3 (continued)

	Including Medical Schools			Excluding Medical Schools		Change in Rank of State
Total		21,352	Total		11,741	
Rank	State	Amount	Rank	State	Amount	
46	Montana[a]	56	46	Idaho[a]	34	3
47	Delaware	48	47	North Dakota[a]	33	1
48	North Dakota[a]	41	48	Arkansas[a]	29	-5
49	Idaho[a]	34	49	Maine[a]	20	1
50	Maine[a]	20	50	Vermont[a]	19	-9
51	Wyoming[a]	18	51	Wyoming[a]	18	0
52	South Dakota[a]	17	52	South Dakota[a]	10	0

NOTE: See Table C.2 in Appendix C for more detailed information.

[a]Participant in NSF's EPSCoR program.

As Figure 2.3 shows, in FY 2002, HHS provided 67 percent of these funds, whereas the National Science Foundation (NSF) provided 11 percent, the Department of Defense (DOD) provided 7 percent, NASA provided 5 percent, the Department of Energy (DOE) provided 4 percent, and the Department of Agriculture (USDA) provided 3 percent. The remainder of the federal R&D funds going to the nation's universities and colleges in FY 2002 came from the departments of Commerce (DOC), Education (DED), Housing and Urban Development (HUD), Interior (DOI), Justice (DOJ), Labor (DOL), Transportation (DOT), and Veterans Affairs (DVA), as well as from the Environmental Protection Agency (EPA), the Nuclear Regulatory Commission (NRC), and

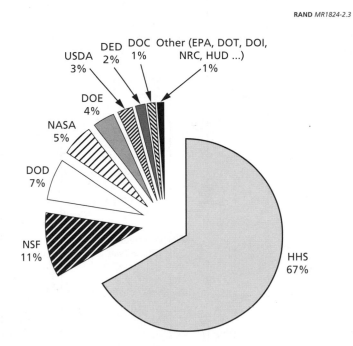

RAND *MR1824-2.3*

Figure 2.3—Funds Provided by Federal Agencies to Universities and Colleges for Conduct of R&D in FY 2002

the Social Security Administration (SSA). By far the largest of these "small providers," as shown in Figure 2.3, were DOC (1 percent), DED (2 percent), DOI (0.2 percent), DOT (0.3 percent), and the EPA (0.6 percent).

Table 2.4 lists the federal R&D funds provided to universities and colleges by the individual agencies in FY 2002. Many of the same states that appear in the top ranks when all the federal R&D funds provided to universities and colleges in FY 2002 are examined (see Tables 2.1 and 2.2) are also in the top ranks of the recipients of R&D funds from one or more of the "major provider" agencies.

Indeed, as shown in Table 2.4, nine of the top ten states whose universities and colleges received the most R&D funds from HHS in FY 2002 were also among the top ten states in the overall ranking of federal R&D funds universities and colleges received in FY 2002. Only Ohio dropped out of the top ten states when the R&D funds HHS provided to universities and colleges in FY 2002 were considered alone, displaced by Missouri, which rose to tenth place in HHS's ranking from twelfth place in the overall state ranking (see Tables 2.1 and 2.2).

The rankings of the top states changed a bit more for the other federal agencies that provided substantial R&D funds to universities and colleges. For example, Florida and Washington were among the top ten of those states whose universities and colleges received the most R&D funds from NSF in FY 2002, displacing North Carolina, and Ohio, which were in the overall top ten. Similarly, Florida was among the top ten whose universities and colleges received the most R&D funds from DOD in FY 2002, displacing Michigan, which was in the overall top ten. Alabama, Colorado, Florida, and Virginia were among the top ten of those states whose universities and colleges received the most R&D funds from NASA in FY 2002, displacing Illinois, Michigan, North Carolina, and Ohio, which were in the overall top ten. Florida, Georgia, and Wisconsin were among the top ten whose universities and colleges received the most R&D funds from DOE in FY 2002, displacing Maryland, North Carolina, and Ohio, which were in the overall top ten. And finally, Florida, Georgia, Iowa, and Mississippi were among the top ten whose universities and colleges received the most R&D funds from USDA in FY 2002, displacing Illinois, Maryland, Massachusetts, and Ohio, which were in the overall top ten. Only California, New York, Pennsylvania, and Texas made the top ten regardless of which federal agency's R&D funding was examined. Indeed, California ranked first in every agency except DOD and NASA, where it ranked second.

In short, the universities and colleges in only four states (California, New York, Pennsylvania, and Texas) were successful in obtaining significant amounts of R&D funds from *all* the major federal R&D agencies. For most states, however, the success of their institutions of higher education in obtaining these funds from the six major federal R&D agencies varied widely for the different agencies. Indeed, the ranking of the average state's universities and colleges varied by almost 20 places in terms of total R&D funds received in FY 2002 from each major federal R&D agency. That is, the institutions of higher education in most states appeared to "specialize" in conducting the R&D that only one or two of the major federal R&D agencies funded, rather than engaging in the entire range of R&D for all federal agencies.

Table 2.4

Agencies Providing Federal Funds to Universities and Colleges, Including Medical Schools, for Conduct of R&D in FY 2002, by State in Rank Order (Obligations in Millions)

	HHS			NSF			DOD			NASA			DOE			USDA			Other		
	State	Amount	%	State	Amount	%	State	Amount	%	State	Amount	%	State	Amount	%	State	Amount	%	State	Amount	%
Total		14,214	66.6		2,355	11.0		1,473	6.9		1,101	5.2		809	3.8		539	2.5		860	4.0
Rank																					
1	CA	1,770	64.9	CA	397	14.5	MD	257	19.7	MD	235	18.0	CA	104	3.8	CA	30	1.1	CA	76	2.8
2	NY	1,288	77.1	IL	160	19.5	CA	187	6.9	CA	162	6.0	MA	86	7.2	TX	23	1.9	CO	41	9.4
3	PA	963	72.6	NY	155	9.3	PA	145	11.0	CO	59	13.6	NY	72	4.3	NC	20	2.3	NY	40	2.4
4	TX	922	73.4	MA	137	11.4	TX	96	7.7	TX	48	3.8	TX	38	3.0	IA	20	7.9	MA	39	3.3
5	MA	808	67.5	PA	108	8.1	MA	73	6.1	MA	45	3.8	PA	32	2.4	MI	19	2.9	TX	38	3.1
6	MD	688	52.8	MI	104	15.7	NY	61	3.6	AL	40	10.4	IL	29	3.6	GA	18	3.8	FL	35	7.0
7	NC	684	79.7	TX	91	7.2	IL	57	7.0	FL	36	7.3	MI	26	4.0	NY	18	1.1	MD	34	2.6
8	IL	524	64.1	WA	76	13.1	OH	46	7.8	NY	36	2.1	WI	26	5.6	MS	17	13.9	NC	33	3.9
9	FL	441	66.9	FL	74	15.0	FL	46	9.3	VA	31	8.1	FL	26	5.2	PA	16	1.2	PA	32	2.4
10	MO	439	84.7	MD	67	5.1	NC	37	4.3	PA	31	2.3	GA	26	5.2	FL	16	3.2	NH	30	21.8
11	WA	415	72.0	GA	64	13.1	GA	36	7.3	UT	25	11.7	NV	24	40.5	OH	15	2.6	OR	28	9.8
12	OH	415	70.6	AZ	64	25.4	MS	29	23.2	HI	25	18.3	AL	22	5.8	AL	15	3.8	VA	25	6.6
13	MN	364	78.4	VA	59	15.3	MI	28	4.3	OH	24	4.0	WA	22	3.9	WI	14	3.0	MI	25	3.8
14	CT	353	85.3	IN	59	20.6	NM	28	20.9	AZ	20	7.8	SC	20	11.7	MN	14	3.0	IL	21	2.6
15	WI	320	68.4	CO	57	13.2	NJ	26	8.3	GA	18	3.7	IN	19	6.6	IL	13	1.6	WI	21	4.4
16	GA	313	64.0	NC	57	6.6	VA	25	6.5	WV	18	25.3	NC	15	1.7	MO	13	2.5	OH	20	3.4
17	TN	302	78.8	NJ	56	17.7	WI	23	4.9	MI	16	2.5	NJ	14	4.5	VA	13	3.3	AK	19	32.6
18	AL	273	70.5	OH	55	9.4	WA	23	3.9	AK	13	23.0	MD	13	1.0	WA	13	2.2	WA	19	3.2
19	FL	260	52.9	WI	53	11.4	AZ	22	8.8	IL	13	1.6	OH	13	2.2	KY	12	7.7	HI	18	13.5
20	CO	245	56.5	MN	43	9.2	DC	18	8.5	NJ	13	4.1	CO	12	2.8	ND	11	26.9	SC	17	10.3
21	VA	221	57.2	OR	39	13.7	HI	18	13.6	OK	12	10.5	WV	12	16.9	NE	11	11.0	MS	17	13.6
22	OR	189	65.8	TN	28	7.3	IN	18	6.1	NC	12	1.4	VA	12	3.1	AR	11	15.3	NJ	15	4.8
23	NJ	182	58.1	MO	25	4.9	UT	17	7.8	MO	11	2.2	NM	11	8.3	TN	10	2.7	CT	15	3.6
24	IA	171	69.2	UT	25	11.5	MN	16	3.5	NH	11	8.2	CT	11	2.6	IN	10	3.5	GA	14	2.8
25	IN	164	57.5	IA	25	10.0	NE	15	14.8	MS	11	8.7	MN	10	2.1	OR	10	3.4	DC	13	6.1
26	DC	162	74.7	HI	20	14.7	RI	14	13.6	WI	11	2.3	MS	10	7.6	LA	9	5.3	RI	13	12.4
27	UT	130	60.5	NM	18	13.8	TN	13	3.5	IA	10	3.9	MO	9	1.6	MD	9	0.7	MN	12	2.7
28	AZ	122	48.6	CT	18	4.3	AL	13	3.3	MT	10	17.0	KS	8	7.1	CO	9	2.0	AL	12	3.2
29	LA	117	65.4	SC	17	10.2	MO	12	2.3	TN	9	2.5	AZ	8	3.2	OK	9	7.2	TN	12	3.1

Table 2.4 (continued)

Rank	HHS			NSF			DOD			NASA			DOE			USDA			Other		
		Amount	%		Amount	%		Amount	%		Amount	%		Amount	%		Amount	%		Amount	%
30	KY	108	72.1	KS	17	14.0	CO	11	2.6	WA	9	1.6	TN	8	2.1	MA	8	0.7	IA	11	4.5
31	SC	99	59.0	LA	16	8.9	LA	9	5.2	LA	9	5.0	IA	8	3.1	SC	8	4.9	LA	11	6.1
32	NH	77	55.6	RI	15	14.7	CT	8	1.9	NM	8	6.3	LA	8	4.2	NJ	8	2.6	WV	10	14.7
33	KS	74	61.6	OK	13	11.2	OR	8	2.7	IN	8	2.9	UT	8	3.5	MT	8	14.3	OK	10	8.3
34	PR	67	75.7	NH	13	9.3	OK	5	4.4	DC	8	3.6	OR	7	2.5	KS	8	6.5	AZ	9	3.7
35	OK	64	54.1	KY	13	8.5	KY	4	2.6	ID	7	19.6	ND	6	15.0	UT	8	3.5	MO	9	1.7
36	VT	61	82.8	DE	12	25.7	IA	3	1.4	OR	6	2.2	OK	5	4.3	WV	7	9.9	IN	8	2.8
37	NM	61	45.7	AL	12	3.1	MT	3	6.0	PR	5	5.7	DC	5	2.3	AZ	7	2.6	KY	8	5.1
38	NE	54	55.0	NV	11	19.0	NH	3	2.2	RI	5	4.7	KY	3	2.3	ID	6	17.1	KS	7	6.2
39	RI	51	49.3	NE	10	10.0	SC	3	1.7	MN	5	1.0	RI	3	2.8	VT	6	7.6	NE	5	5.0
40	AR	48	69.0	DC	9	4.3	KS	3	2.3	CT	5	2.3	AK	3	5.0	SD	5	31.1	ME	4	19.8
41	HI	46	34.5	AK	8	14.4	AK	2	4.2	ND	5	11.4	DE	3	5.4	CT	5	1.2	DE	4	8.2
42	MS	33	26.8	MT	8	14.6	WV	2	3.3	SC	4	2.2	NE	2	2.5	HI	5	3.7	ND	4	9.4
43	DE	22	46.6	MS	8	6.3	NV	2	3.5	KS	3	2.2	ID	2	6.8	AK	4	7.7	WY	3	17.6
44	MT	22	39.6	ME	8	37.8	ME	2	8.6	KY	3	1.7	HI	2	1.6	PR	4	5.0	NV	3	5.2
45	WV	19	26.9	PR	7	7.9	DE	2	3.6	NV	2	2.7	MT	2	3.3	ME	4	20.4	AR	3	4.4
46	NV	15	24.5	AR	6	8.5	PR	1	1.7	NE	2	1.6	NH	1	0.9	NM	4	3.0	PR	3	3.4
47	ND	11	28.1	ID	5	15.6	ND	1	2.5	DE	1	2.7	VT	1	1.7	DE	4	7.8	MT	3	5.3
48	ID	11	32.7	WY	5	26.7	AR	1	1.2	VT	1	1.5	PR	1	0.7	NV	3	4.6	UT	3	1.4
49	SD	8	44.1	VT	4	4.8	SD	0	2.4	WY	1	5.2	WY	1	2.8	RI	3	2.6	ID	3	8.1
50	AK	8	13.2	ND	3	6.8	WY	0	0.2	SD	1	5.3	AR	0	0.6	NH	3	1.9	NM	3	1.9
51	WY	6	34.3	WV	2	3.1	ID	0	0.0	AR	1	1.1	ME	0	1.3	WY	2	13.3	VT	1	1.6
52	ME	2	10.4	SD	2	12.1	VT	0	0.0	ME	0	1.7	SD	0	0.0	DC	1	0.4	SD	1	5.1

NOTE: See Table C.3 in Appendix C for more detailed information.

A LEVEL PLAYING FIELD

Given that HHS provided over 95 percent of all the R&D funds going to medical schools in FY 2002 (see Figure 2.4), we anticipated that removing the medical school funding from the analysis would change the state rankings in terms of R&D dollars received from HHS. Such was not the case, however, as Table 2.5 shows.

Specifically, nine of the ten states whose institutions of higher education received the most R&D funds from HHS when medical school funding was included in the analysis also received the most when it was excluded (see Tables 2.4 and 2.5). That is, in alphabetical (not rank) order, California, Illinois, Maryland, Massachusetts, Michigan, New York, North Carolina, Pennsylvania, and Texas were home to the institutions of higher education that received the most R&D funds from HHS in FY 2002—regardless of whether the R&D funds for their medical schools were included. Only Missouri dropped out of the top ten ranking when medical schools were excluded, a drop which, as noted previously, indicates that the share of Missouri's federally supported university-based R&D activities based in its medical schools was larger than that of the other top ten states.

Given that less than 5 percent of the federal R&D funds going to medical schools in FY 2002 came from agencies other than HHS, it is not surprising that the states in the top ten rankings for the other major federal R&D agencies—NSF, DOD, NASA, DOE, and USDA (Table 2.5)—are virtually the same after the federal R&D funds going to the medical schools are excluded. Indeed, the specific rankings in the top ten are identical for all but two agencies: DOD, in which case New York and Illinois trade sixth and seventh place, and Georgia and North Carolina trade tenth and eleventh; and NASA, in which case Texas and Massachusetts trade fourth and fifth place, and Florida and New York trade seventh and eighth.

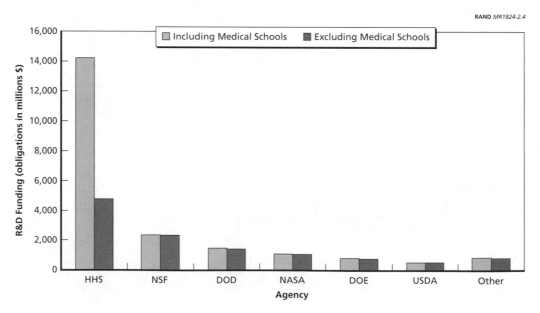

Figure 2.4—Agencies Providing Federal Funds to Universities and Colleges for Conduct of R&D in FY 2002

Table 2.5

Agencies Providing Federal Funds to Universities and Colleges, Excluding Medical Schools, for Conduct of R&D in FY 2002, by State in Rank Order (Obligations in Millions)

	HHS			NSF			DOD			NASA			DOE			USDA			Other		
		Amount	%		Amount	%		Amount	%		Amount	%		Amount	%		Amount	%		Amount	%
Total		4,762	40.6		2,344	20.0		1,407	12.0		1,081	9.2		789	6.7		537	4.6		820	7.0
Rank																					
1	CA	622	39.4	CA	397	25.1	MD	256	30.4	MD	228	27.1	CA	104	6.6	CA	30	1.9	CA	76	4.7
2	MA	441	53.3	IL	160	35.3	CA	187	11.8	CA	162	10.3	MA	85	10.3	TX	22	3.9	CO	41	7.4
3	NY	356	49.5	NY	154	21.4	PA	142	23.5	CO	59	21.4	NY	72	10.0	NC	20	6.0	MA	39	7.4
4	TX	280	48.9	MA	136	16.5	TX	80	14.0	MA	44	5.4	TX	36	6.3	IA	20	15.5	NY	35	32.6
5	PA	246	40.8	PA	108	17.9	MA	72	8.7	TX	43	7.5	PA	31	5.2	MI	19	5.0	FL	35	5.7
6	MD	237	28.1	MI	104	27.1	IL	53	11.7	AL	40	18.6	IL	28	6.2	GA	18	6.3	NC	33	14.7
7	NC	171	50.8	TX	88	15.3	NY	49	6.9	NY	35	4.9	MI	26	6.9	NY	18	2.5	MD	32	15.3
8	WA	164	50.5	WA	76	23.2	OH	46	16.9	FL	32	10.1	WI	26	9.5	MS	17	15.4	NH	30	4.8
9	IL	164	36.3	FL	74	23.0	FL	46	14.2	VA	31	14.6	FL	26	8.0	PA	16	2.7	PA	30	9.9
10	MI	164	42.9	MD	67	8.0	GA	36	12.3	PA	30	5.0	GA	25	8.7	FL	16	4.9	OR	28	6.3
11	WI	130	47.1	GA	64	21.9	NC	29	8.6	UT	25	20.8	NV	22	46.2	OH	15	5.6	VA	25	18.7
12	GA	118	40.5	AZ	64	34.4	MS	29	26.1	HI	25	19.9	AL	22	10.3	AL	15	6.8	MI	25	5.7
13	MN	107	54.1	VA	59	27.6	MI	28	7.4	OH	23	8.5	WA	22	6.9	WI	14	5.2	TX	23	6.1
14	AL	103	47.3	IN	59	29.8	NM	28	28.2	AZ	20	10.6	IN	19	9.5	MN	14	7.1	IL	21	7.8
15	OH	100	36.8	NC	57	16.9	VA	24	11.2	WV	18	31.0	NC	14	4.2	IL	13	3.0	WI	20	8.7
16	FL	93	29.0	CO	56	20.4	NJ	23	11.0	GA	16	5.6	MD	13	1.6	MO	13	8.1	OH	20	8.9
17	CO	88	32.0	OH	55	20.2	WA	23	6.9	MI	16	4.2	OH	13	4.7	VA	13	6.0	AK	19	9.1
18	NJ	87	41.3	NJ	54	25.9	AZ	22	11.9	AK	13	23.0	SC	12	15.4	WA	13	3.9	WA	19	18.1
19	MO	84	51.9	WI	53	19.3	WI	21	7.7	IL	13	2.8	CO	12	4.4	KY	12	16.8	HI	18	10.8
20	DC	80	59.5	MN	43	21.6	HI	18	14.8	NJ	13	6.0	WV	12	20.7	ND	11	33.6	MS	17	5.0
21	IN	76	38.4	OR	39	23.2	DC	18	13.4	OK	12	14.4	NJ	12	5.7	NE	11	16.2	GA	14	11.3
22	OR	71	41.9	TN	28	18.7	IN	18	8.9	NC	12	3.7	VA	12	5.5	AR	11	36.3	DC	13	5.5
23	TN	70	47.2	MO	25	15.4	UT	16	13.4	MO	11	7.0	NM	11	11.2	TN	10	7.0	NJ	13	4.1
24	LA	63	51.0	UT	25	20.5	NE	15	21.8	NH	11	14.7	CT	11	9.4	IN	10	5.1	RI	13	11.2
25	CT	62	54.0	IA	25	19.6	RI	14	20.6	MS	11	9.8	MN	10	5.0	OR	10	5.7	AL	12	9.0
26	AZ	56	30.3	HI	20	15.9	AL	13	5.8	WI	11	3.9	MS	10	8.6	LA	9	7.6	MN	12	7.4
27	IA	51	40.2	NM	18	18.3	MO	12	7.5	IA	10	7.6	KS	8	10.3	MD	9	1.1	TN	12	19.8

Table 2.5 (continued)

Rank	HHS			NSF			DOD			NASA			DOE			USDA			Other		
		Amount	%		Amount	%		Amount	%		Amount	%		Amount	%		Amount	%		Amount	%
28	VA	50	23.2	CT	17	14.9	TN	12	7.8	MT	10	17.0	AZ	8	4.3	CO	9	3.1	IA	11	8.2
29	KS	38	45.3	SC	17	21.1	CO	10	3.8	WA	9	2.9	TN	8	5.3	MA	8	1.0	LA	11	11.7
30	UT	37	30.5	KS	16	19.9	LA	9	7.5	TN	9	6.2	IA	8	6.0	OK	8	9.4	CT	11	17.6
31	HI	36	29.0	LA	15	12.5	OR	8	4.5	LA	9	7.2	MO	8	4.6	NJ	8	3.8	WV	10	6.5
32	OK	34	38.9	RI	15	22.3	MN	7	3.7	NM	8	8.5	UT	7	6.1	MT	8	14.3	OK	9	6.3
33	SC	28	34.9	OK	13	15.0	CT	6	5.3	IN	8	4.2	OR	7	4.3	SC	8	10.1	AZ	9	5.3
34	NM	27	27.2	NH	13	16.6	OK	5	6.0	DC	8	5.8	LA	7	5.3	KS	8	9.4	SC	9	2.4
35	KY	27	38.9	KY	13	18.6	KY	4	5.7	ID	7	19.6	ND	6	18.6	UT	8	6.3	MO	9	9.7
36	PR	27	55.2	DE	12	25.7	MT	3	6.0	OR	6	3.7	DC	5	3.8	WV	7	12.1	IN	8	8.1
37	NE	23	33.9	AL	12	5.5	NH	3	3.9	PR	5	10.4	OK	5	5.4	AZ	7	3.5	KY	8	2.5
38	DE	22	46.6	NV	11	23.6	IA	3	2.3	RI	5	7.1	KY	3	5.0	ID	6	17.1	KS	7	6.1
39	MT	22	39.6	NE	10	14.7	KS	3	3.3	MN	5	2.4	RI	3	4.2	VT	6	29.7	NE	5	8.4
40	MS	20	17.8	DC	9	6.9	AK	2	4.2	ND	5	14.2	AK	3	5.0	SD	5	51.5	ME	4	4.7
41	NH	16	20.8	AK	8	14.4	WV	2	4.1	CT	4	3.0	DE	3	5.4	CT	5	4.3	DE	4	7.4
42	RI	16	23.3	MT	8	14.6	SC	2	2.8	SC	3	4.4	NE	2	3.7	HI	5	4.0	ND	4	7.4
43	ID	11	32.7	ME	8	37.8	NV	2	4.3	KY	3	3.8	ID	2	6.8	AK	4	7.7	WY	3	32.6
44	AR	8	28.7	MS	8	6.9	ME	2	8.6	KS	2	2.9	HI	2	1.7	PR	4	9.1	NV	3	5.7
45	AK	8	13.2	PR	7	14.5	DE	2	3.6	NV	2	3.4	MT	2	3.3	ME	4	20.4	PR	3	14.7
46	WY	6	34.3	AR	6	18.9	PR	1	3.0	NE	2	2.3	NH	1	1.6	NM	4	4.1	MT	3	15.3
47	VT	6	32.7	ID	5	15.6	ND	1	3.1	DE	1	2.7	VT	1	6.5	DE	4	7.8	UT	3	4.8
48	WV	6	10.3	WY	5	26.7	AR	1	2.5	VT	1	6.0	PR	1	1.3	NV	3	5.7	AR	3	9.9
49	NV	5	10.2	VT	4	18.9	SD	0	3.9	WY	1	5.2	WY	1	2.8	RI	3	3.9	ID	3	6.3
50	ND	3	10.4	ND	3	8.4	WY	0	0.2	SD	1	8.8	AR	0	1.4	NH	3	3.4	NM	3	18.7
51	ME	2	10.4	WV	2	3.8	ID	0	0.0	AR	1	2.5	ME	0	1.3	WY	2	13.3	VT	1	5.7
52	SD	1	7.4	SD	2	20.1	VT	0	0.0	ME	0	1.7	DC	0	0.0	DC	1	0.7	SD	1	6.1

NOTE: See Table C.5 in Appendix C for more detailed information.

Worthy of particular note is the fact that, even after all the R&D funds going to medical schools were removed from the mix, HHS continued to be *the* major provider of R&D funds to the nation's universities and colleges, supplying 40.6 percent of all such funds in FY 2002 (see Figure 2.4). NSF remained the second largest provider, supplying 20.0 percent of R&D funds to the nation's universities and colleges in FY 2002. DOD remained in third place, providing 12.0 percent. It was followed by NASA, at 9.2 percent; DOE, at 6.7 percent; and USDA, at 4.6 percent. The remaining funds (7.0 percent) were from DOC, DED, HUD, DOI, DOJ, DOL, DOT, DVA, and the EPA, NRC, and SSA in various small amounts.

R&D SPECIALIZATION AND ITS CONSEQUENCES

As with the agency-by-agency state rankings that include the federal R&D funds going to the medical schools at universities and colleges, only the institutions of higher education in California, New York, Pennsylvania, and Texas were successful in obtaining significant R&D funds from all major federal R&D agencies when we excluded the R&D funds going to medical schools. Similarly, the ranking of the universities and colleges of the average state also varied 20 places in terms of the total R&D funds received in FY 2002 from each major federal R&D agency. This provides additional support for the notion that the institutions of higher education in most states appear to "specialize" in conducting the type of R&D that is funded by only one or two of the major federal R&D agencies.

Table 2.6 provides a different view of the information in Table 2.5, this one organized by state instead of rank. In so doing, it shows that the major sources of federal R&D funding vary considerably from state to state. Specifically, Table 2.6 shows that HHS is not the primary source of federal R&D funds for the universities and colleges in over 25 percent of the states. Similarly, it shows that NSF is not the secondary source of such funds in over 40 percent of the states, and DOD is not the tertiary source in over 75 percent of the states. In short, Table 2.6 shows that the relationship between the universities and colleges within a particular state and the federal agencies that give them R&D funds is quite individualized. The numerous ways in which the federally supported R&D activities of the universities and colleges within the various states differ from one another is a topic that, given its considerable breadth, must be left for a future RaDiUS-based report. For now, we will simply note that the universities and colleges that reside in the various states tend to "specialize" in the R&D funded by specific federal agencies and that the consequences of this, which we discuss below, may not be trivial.

HOW FEDERAL R&D FUNDS ARE CONVEYED

One of the consequences of "specialization" is that the legal "ground rules" for conducting federally funded R&D at the universities and colleges may vary considerably from one state to the next. Specifically, HHS, NSF, and USDA fund the vast majority of their extramural R&D activities via grants (either project grants or formula grants), regardless of recipient. In contrast, DOD and NASA fund the vast majority of their

Table 2.6

Agencies Providing the First, Second, and Third Most Federal Funds to Universities and Colleges, Excluding Medical Schools, for Conduct of R&D in FY 2002, by State

| State | Rank | | | | | | | | |
	HHS	NSF	DOD	NASA	DOE	USDA	EDUC	DOC	Other
AK		Third		First			Second		
AL	First			Second	Third				
AR	Second	Third				First			
AZ	Second	First	Third						
CA	First	Second	Third						
CO	First	Third		Second					
CT	First	Second			Third				
DC	First		Second						Third
DE	First	Second				Third			
FL	First	Second	Third						
GA	First	Second	Third						
HI	First	Third		Second					
IA	First	Second				Third			
ID	First			Second		Third			
IL	First	Second	Third						
IN	First	Second			Third				
KS	First	Second			Third				
KY	First	Second				Third			
LA	First	Second				Third			
MA	First	Second			Third				
MD	Second		First	Third					
ME	Third	First				Second			
MI	First	Second	Third						
MN	First	Second				Third			
MO	First	Second				Third			
MS	Second		First			Third			
MT	First	Third		Second					
NC	First	Second	Third						
ND				Third	Second	First			
NE	First		Second			Third			
NH	Second	Third					First		
NJ	First	Second	Third						
NM	Second	Third	First						
NV	Third	Second			First				
NY	First	Second			Third				
OH	First	Second	Third						
OK	First	Second		Third					
OR	First	Second							Third
PA	First	Third	Second						
PR	First	Second		Third					
RI	First	Second	Third						
SC	First	Second			Third				
SD		Second		Third		First			
TN	First	Second	Third						
TX	First	Second	Third						
UT	First	Third		Second					
VA	Second	First		Third					
VT	First	Third				Second			
WA	First	Second	Third						
WI	First	Second			Third				
WV				First	Second			Third	
WY	First	Second							Third

NOTE: See Table C.6 in Appendix C for more detailed information.

extramural R&D activities via contracts, regardless of recipient. DOE also funds the majority of its extramural R&D activities via contracts. The R&D dollars DOE conveys via contracts, however, go largely to universities, corporations, and/or nonprofits for the management and operation of the national laboratories, which this analysis does not include. As a result, the DOE extramural funding profile of relevance to this discussion is more balanced with regard to the use of grants and contracts.

That is, when one looks at the federal R&D dollars going only to universities and colleges, the funding profiles of DOD and NASA are quite different from those of HHS, NSF, and USDA, with respect to the mix of grants and contracts. In FY 2002, over 45 percent of the R&D funds that DOD awarded to universities and colleges and over 34 percent of the R&D funds NASA awarded to universities and colleges were conveyed via contracts, whereas HHS, NSF, and USDA conveyed less than 4 percent of their R&D funds to universities and colleges via contracts. Consequently, universities and colleges that receive a large share of their federal funds for R&D from HHS, NSF, and USDA have more freedom to conduct that R&D, because the federal government has little control over R&D conducted with funds conveyed via grants. In addition, these universities and colleges have fewer concerns about rights that the federal government may have to the data or other intellectual property resulting from their R&D, because such rights attach only to federal R&D funds conveyed to universities and colleges via contracts.[1]

The majority (78.3 percent) of federal R&D funds going to universities and colleges were conveyed in the form of project grants, as shown in Table 2.7. However, the proportion of the total federal R&D funds going to institutions of higher education in each state in the form of project grants varied considerably. For example, among the top ten states whose universities and colleges (including their medical schools) received the most overall federal funds for the conduct of R&D in FY 2002, New York received 88.0 percent of its funds in the form of project grants, whereas Maryland received only 54.2 percent of its funds in this form. Despite this range, however, nine of the ten states whose universities and colleges received the most overall federal R&D funds (see left side of Table 2.3) were the same states whose universities and colleges received the most federal R&D funds via project grants. Only Ohio fell out of the top ten ranking of recipients of project grants, replaced by Washington.

After project grants, cooperative agreements are the second most common vehicle for transferring R&D funds from the federal government to the universities and colleges in the states. Specifically, Table 2.7 shows that 13.2 percent of all R&D funds going to such institutions in FY 2002 took the form of cooperative agreements. This fund-transferring vehicle is similar to a project grant in that both are designed to transfer the "discovery" work to the nonfederal recipient of the funds, but it differs from a project grant in that it requires the federal funding unit to participate more actively in the actual conduct of the R&D. Consequently, it is not surprising to find

---

[1] See 35 USC 200 et seq., the provisions of which are commonly referred to as Bayh-Dole. Also see 48 CFR 27.400 et seq.

Table 2.7

Federal Funds Provided to Universities and Colleges, Including Medical Schools, for Conduct of R&D in FY 2002 , by State in Rank Order (Obligations in Millions)

	Project Grants			Contracts			Cooperative Agreements			Formula Grants		
		Amount	%		Amount	%		Amount	%		Amount	%
Total		16,717	78.3		1,568	7.3		2,825	13.2		242	1.1
Rank												
1	CA	2,158	79.2	MD	445	34.1	CA	402	14.8	TX	11	0.9
2	NY	1,469	88.0	CA	160	5.9	MA	251	21.0	NC	11	1.3
3	PA	1,066	80.4	PA	115	8.7	TX	210	16.7	DC	10	4.7
4	TX	946	75.4	TX	89	7.1	NY	159	9.5	AL	9	2.4
5	MA	905	75.7	OH	58	9.9	MD	148	11.4	TN	8	2.1
6	MD	706	54.2	NC	53	6.2	PA	139	10.5	GA	8	1.6
7	NC	677	78.9	UT	44	20.6	IL	119	14.6	KY	8	5.4
8	IL	658	80.5	FL	39	7.9	NC	117	13.7	MO	8	1.5
9	MI	548	83.2	AL	39	10.0	MO	102	19.7	VA	7	1.9
10	WA	486	84.2	CO	38	8.8	MI	82	12.4	MS	7	5.5
11	OH	468	79.7	MA	38	3.2	AL	76	19.7	PA	7	0.5
12	FL	397	80.9	MO	37	7.2	DC	70	32.1	IA	6	2.6
13	WI	396	84.5	NY	36	2.2	CO	65	15.1	AR	6	8.8
14	GA	395	80.8	IL	35	4.2	WA	64	11.1	NY	6	0.4
15	CT	388	93.7	GA	33	6.7	MN	63	13.6	OH	6	1.0
16	MO	372	71.7	MS	27	21.5	OH	55	9.4	CA	6	0.2
17	MN	369	79.5	MN	27	5.8	GA	53	10.9	IL	6	0.7
18	CO	327	75.4	HI	24	17.9	VA	53	13.6	MI	6	0.8
19	VA	311	80.5	WI	24	5.0	TN	50	13.0	FL	6	1.1
20	TN	306	79.8	MI	23	3.5	FL	49	10.1	WI	5	1.2
21	NJ	269	85.7	WA	23	3.9	WI	43	9.3	MN	5	1.2
22	AL	263	67.9	TN	19	5.1	AZ	32	12.6	SC	5	3.2
23	OR	250	87.0	DC	16	7.3	LA	31	17.4	IN	5	1.8
24	IN	242	85.0	VA	15	4.0	OK	28	23.8	LA	5	2.9
25	IA	225	91.4	NJ	14	4.6	NJ	27	8.7	OK	5	4.2
26	AZ	208	83.1	AK	12	20.8	OR	26	9.1	WA	4	0.8
27	UT	149	69.1	IN	12	4.1	IN	26	9.1	PR	4	4.5
28	LA	138	76.9	AZ	9	3.4	HI	25	18.8	WV	4	5.6
29	SC	137	81.7	NM	8	5.8	SC	24	14.6	MD	4	0.3
30	KY	133	88.7	OR	7	2.6	NM	21	15.8	OR	4	1.2
31	DC	121	55.9	RI	6	5.8	WV	21	29.2	KS	4	3.0
32	NH	116	83.9	NV	6	9.8	UT	20	9.5	NE	4	3.5
33	KS	105	88.3	CT	6	1.4	MS	20	16.2	CO	3	0.7
34	NM	103	77.0	OK	5	4.3	PR	19	21.7	NJ	3	0.9
35	NE	87	87.9	LA	5	2.8	CT	18	4.4	SD	3	14.8
36	RI	85	82.2	IA	4	1.7	NH	17	12.2	ID	3	7.5
37	HI	83	62.1	NH	4	2.6	NV	14	23.7	DE	3	5.3
38	OK	80	67.8	WY	3	15.2	AK	14	24.1	MT	2	4.4
39	MS	71	56.8	KY	2	1.5	RI	11	10.7	ND	2	6.0
40	PR	65	73.1	ME	2	11.0	IA	11	4.3	MA	2	0.2
41	VT	64	87.0	VT	2	2.3	KS	9	7.9	ME	2	11.5
42	AR	61	87.7	WV	1	1.4	NE	8	8.3	AZ	2	0.9
43	MT	52	92.9	KS	1	0.8	ND	7	16.6	CT	2	0.5
44	WV	46	63.8	SC	1	0.5	KY	7	4.4	UT	2	0.9
45	DE	43	89.2	MT	1	1.1	VT	6	8.4	NM	2	1.4
46	NV	39	64.4	PR	1	0.7	DE	2	5.1	WY	2	9.6
47	ND	31	77.4	NE	0	0.3	AR	2	3.1	NH	2	1.3
48	AK	30	52.7	AR	0	0.4	WY	2	10.7	VT	2	2.3
49	ID	30	89.1	DE	0	0.5	ID	1	3.1	HI	1	1.1
50	ME	16	77.0	ID	0	0.4	MT	1	1.5	AK	1	2.4
51	SD	15	84.1	ND	0	0.0	SD	0	1.2	RI	1	1.2
52	WY	12	64.5	SD	0	0.0	ME	0	0.5	NV	1	2.1

NOTE: See Table C.7 in Appendix C for more detailed information.

that nine of the states whose institutions of higher education received the most federal R&D funds in the form of cooperative agreements are also among the top ten states that received the most federal R&D funds in the form of project grants. Only Washington fell out of the top ten ranking of recipients of cooperative agreements, replaced by Missouri.

In substantial contrast, however, is the pattern among the ten states whose universities and colleges received the most federal R&D funds in the form of contracts. Only six of the states in this group (California, Maryland, North Carolina, Ohio, Pennsylvania, and Texas) were also among the top ten states whose universities and colleges received the most overall federal R&D funds. Not surprisingly, all of the states in the group that received the most federal R&D funds in the form of contracts—the four new "top ten" states (Alabama, Colorado, Florida, and Utah), as well as the six "seasoned top ten" states—were home to sizable DOD, NASA, and/or DOE facilities. Indeed, the ten states whose universities and colleges received the largest percentage, as opposed to the largest amount, of their federal R&D funds in FY 2002 in the form of contracts (in descending order: Maryland, Mississippi, Alaska, Utah, Hawaii, Wyoming, Maine, Alabama, Ohio, and Nevada) were home to four of NASA's flight and/or research centers, five directorates of DOD's Air Force Research Laboratory, three major field sites of DOD's Navy Research Laboratory, two laboratory/research centers of DOD's Army Research Laboratory, DOD's major research facility for testing chemical and biological weapons, and DOE's Nevada Test Site. Presumably, some amount of the federal R&D conducted by the institutions of higher education in these states was somehow related to the work of these nearby federal R&D units.

Formula grants, which are used in very limited circumstances and primarily by only one federal agency (USDA) to fund R&D, were not used to transfer many R&D dollars to institutions of higher education in any state in FY 2002 (the total was 1.3 percent). Given that formula grants are not awarded in full and open competition but, instead, generally carry mandatory minimum funding amounts for each eligible state, it is not surprising that the states whose institutions received the largest share of their federal R&D dollars in the form of formula grants in FY 2002 are also among the states with the fewest and the smallest universities and colleges (Arizona, Idaho, Maine, Mississippi, North Dakota, South Dakota, West Virginia, and Wyoming, all of which received more than 6.0 percent of their federal R&D dollars in the form of formula grants in FY 2002).

Table 2.8 shows that removing the federal R&D funds going to medical schools from the analysis has very little effect on the pattern among the states. With medical school funding excluded, the same ten states remained at the top of the ranks of states whose universities and colleges received the most federal R&D funds via project grants and formula grants (albeit in a slightly different order for project grants). In addition, nine of the ten states that had topped the ranks of states whose universities and colleges received the most federal R&D funds via contracts remained at the top, as did eight of the ten states that had topped the ranks of states whose universities and colleges received the most federal R&D funds via cooperative agreements. Thus, while the exclusion of medical schools affected the relative mix of grants and

Table 2.8

Federal Funds Provided to Universities and Colleges, Excluding Medical Schools, for Conduct of R&D in FY 2002, by State in Rank Order (Obligations in Millions)

	Project Grants			Contracts			Cooperative Agreements			Formula Grants		
		Amount	%		Amount	%		Amount	%		Amount	%
Total		8,360	71.2		1,431	12.2		1,708	14.5		242	2.1
Rank												
1	CA	1,157	73.3	MD	435	51.6	CA	258	16.4	TX	11	1.9
2	NY	587	81.6	CA	157	10.0	MA	227	27.5	NC	11	3.2
3	MA	560	67.7	PA	112	18.6	NY	104	14.4	DC	10	7.6
4	TX	428	74.8	TX	62	10.8	MD	95	11.3	AL	9	4.4
5	PA	412	68.2	OH	56	20.6	IL	79	17.5	TN	8	5.4
6	IL	336	74.2	AL	39	17.9	PA	73	12.1	GA	8	2.8
7	MD	309	36.7	MA	37	4.5	TX	72	12.6	KY	8	11.7
8	MI	298	77.9	NC	37	10.9	MI	62	16.2	MO	8	4.8
9	WA	270	82.8	MO	36	22.4	DC	55	40.8	VA	7	3.4
10	NC	256	76.3	FL	36	11.1	AL	45	20.6	MS	7	6.2
11	FL	254	79.0	CO	35	12.6	CO	44	15.9	PA	7	1.1
12	WI	225	81.6	UT	34	28.0	MN	37	18.6	IA	6	5.0
13	GA	219	74.9	IL	32	7.0	VA	37	17.1	AR	6	20.9
14	CO	194	70.4	GA	29	10.0	GA	36	12.3	NY	6	0.8
15	OH	190	69.5	MS	27	24.0	NC	32	9.5	OH	6	2.2
16	NJ	183	87.0	HI	24	19.5	WA	29	8.9	CA	6	0.4
17	IN	168	85.3	WA	23	6.9	OK	27	31.6	IL	6	1.3
18	VA	155	72.5	NY	22	3.1	LA	26	21.1	MI	6	1.5
19	AZ	154	83.6	WI	20	7.3	FL	26	8.1	FL	6	1.7
20	OR	141	83.2	MN	20	9.9	WI	25	9.1	WI	5	2.0
21	MN	136	68.8	MI	17	4.5	HI	23	18.2	MN	5	2.7
22	AL	124	57.1	TN	15	10.1	AZ	21	11.6	SC	5	6.8
23	MO	114	70.0	VA	15	7.0	OH	21	7.7	IN	5	2.6
24	IA	110	87.4	AK	12	20.8	WV	21	35.9	LA	5	4.2
25	TN	106	70.9	IN	12	5.9	TN	20	13.5	OK	5	5.7
26	CT	106	91.5	DC	11	8.5	MS	20	17.8	WA	4	1.3
27	LA	88	71.1	NJ	8	3.8	NM	18	18.1	PR	4	8.3
28	HI	76	61.2	NM	8	7.9	OR	17	10.3	WV	4	6.8
29	UT	75	61.9	OR	7	4.4	NJ	17	7.9	MD	4	0.5
30	KS	73	88.2	AZ	7	3.7	SC	15	19.1	OR	4	2.1
31	NM	71	72.2	RI	6	8.8	NV	14	29.4	KS	4	4.3
32	NH	60	77.1	NV	6	12.2	AK	14	24.1	NE	4	5.2
33	DC	58	43.1	CT	6	5.0	NH	12	16.0	CO	3	1.1
34	SC	58	73.2	OK	5	5.2	IN	12	6.1	NJ	3	1.4
35	MS	57	51.9	LA	4	3.6	PR	11	22.4	SD	3	24.4
36	NE	57	84.8	NH	4	4.6	UT	10	8.6	ID	3	7.5
37	RI	55	79.8	IA	3	2.7	ND	7	20.7	DE	3	5.3
38	KY	54	78.7	WY	3	15.2	RI	7	9.6	MT	2	4.4
39	MT	52	92.9	KY	2	3.3	NE	6	9.6	ND	2	7.5
40	OK	50	57.5	ME	2	11.0	IA	6	4.9	MA	2	0.3
41	DE	43	89.2	VT	2	9.1	KS	6	7.0	ME	2	11.5
42	PR	33	68.1	WV	1	1.7	MO	5	2.8	AZ	2	1.2
43	WV	32	55.6	SC	1	0.9	KY	4	6.3	CT	2	1.8
44	AK	30	52.7	MT	1	1.1	VT	4	19.2	UT	2	1.6
45	ID	30	89.1	PR	1	1.2	DE	2	5.1	NM	2	1.8
46	NV	27	55.8	KS	0	0.6	CT	2	1.7	WY	2	9.6
47	ND	23	71.8	NE	0	0.4	WY	2	10.7	NH	2	2.2
48	AR	22	74.5	AR	0	0.8	AR	1	3.8	VT	2	9.1
49	ME	16	77.0	DE	0	0.5	ID	1	3.1	HI	1	1.2
50	VT	12	62.5	ID	0	0.4	MT	1	1.5	AK	1	2.4
51	WY	12	64.5	ND	0	0.0	SD	0	2.0	RI	1	1.9
52	SD	8	73.6	SD	0	0.0	ME	0	0.5	NV	1	2.6

NOTE: See Table C.8 in Appendix C for more detailed information.

contracts received by universities and colleges in some states, it had little effect on the overall ranking of the states with respect to their receipt of grants and contracts.

WHICH INSTITUTIONS COMPETE FOR FEDERAL R&D FUNDS?

To date, the only universities and colleges commonly discussed in the competition for federal R&D funds are those that were "winners" of such awards. Not all universities and colleges in the nation, however, attempt to compete for federal R&D funds. To determine the percentage of universities and colleges in the states that do successfully compete for federal R&D funds, we identified the "universe" of all potentially eligible institutions in the states and compared it with the institutions that actually obtained such funds in FY 2002.

Not surprisingly, every MD-granting institution in every state sought and obtained federal R&D funds in FY 2002 (see Table 2.9). At least 50 percent of all universities and colleges that grant PhD degrees in all states successfully obtained federal R&D funds in FY 2002. In 38 states, at least 75 percent of the universities and colleges that grant PhD degrees successfully obtained federal R&D funds in FY 2002. The situation for universities and colleges granting master's degrees (both MA's and MS's) and bachelor's degrees (both BA's and BS's) was noticeably different, with many fewer such institutions competing for and/or successfully obtaining such funds. Nevertheless, in 31 states, at least 50 percent of the institutions granting master's degrees successfully obtained federal R&D funds, as did over 50 percent of the institutions granting bachelor's degrees in 21 states. Please note that these percentages need to be used with care, however, because they put all states on an equal footing with respect to the success of their institutions of higher education in obtaining federal R&D funds—regardless of how many such institutions a state has. Thus, for instance, Wyoming's single four-year institution of higher education is put on an equal footing with New York's more than 100 such institutions—many of which have multiple campuses. In addition, institutions with fewer than 100 faculty members and students are treated the same way as institutions with thousands of faculty members and students. Note also that Table 2.9 includes universities and colleges that do not want federal R&D funds and that therefore neither apply for nor receive federal R&D funds. Consequently, states that are home to a number of institutions that confer graduate degrees not involving the conduct of R&D (e.g., doctorates in divinity and/or counseling) will have noticeably lower percentages of institutions obtaining R&D funds. Nevertheless, Table 2.9 does show, for the first time, the proportion of the states' universities and colleges that received R&D funds from the federal government in FY 2002. In so doing, it shows that universities and colleges in every part of the nation are interested in obtaining federal R&D funds.

Table 2.9

Percentage of Universities and Colleges Receiving Federal Funds for Conduct of R&D in FY 2002, by State and by Types of Degrees Granted by the Universities and Colleges Located in the State

State	All Degree Granting Institutions	All BA/BS Granting Institutions	All MA/MS Granting Institutions	All PhD Granting Institutions	All MD Granting Institutions
Alabama	48.6	50.0	56.0	90.0	100.0
Alaska	83.3	83.3	100.0	100.0	na
Arizona	26.7	28.6	28.6	60.0	100.0
Arkansas	42.9	42.9	61.5	100.0	100.0
California	46.2	51.0	50.5	58.3	100.0
Colorado	50.0	50.0	62.5	80.0	100.0
Connecticut	39.1	40.9	47.4	87.5	100.0
Delaware	40.0	40.0	40.0	50.0	na
District of Columbia	61.5	66.7	66.7	100.0	100.0
Florida	40.4	41.2	55.9	87.5	100.0
Georgia	49.0	46.9	55.6	100.0	100.0
Hawaii	33.3	33.3	50.0	100.0	100.0
Idaho	42.9	42.9	60.0	100.0	na
Illinois	36.5	38.6	45.1	54.2	100.0
Indiana	32.6	34.1	29.7	50.0	100.0
Iowa	37.8	37.8	42.9	83.3	100.0
Kansas	30.8	30.8	38.9	100.0	100.0
Kentucky	21.2	21.9	31.8	50.0	100.0
Louisiana	73.9	72.7	78.9	100.0	100.0
Maine	50.0	50.0	44.4	100.0	na
Maryland	59.4	58.1	58.6	84.6	100.0
Massachusetts	44.7	46.4	47.5	77.8	100.0
Michigan	40.4	40.4	48.5	81.8	100.0
Minnesota	38.1	39.5	50.0	54.5	100.0
Mississippi	68.8	68.8	75.0	100.0	100.0
Missouri	28.6	26.7	36.4	70.0	100.0
Montana	60.0	60.0	50.0	100.0	na
Nebraska	22.7	22.7	31.3	100.0	100.0
Nevada	66.7	66.7	100.0	100.0	100.0
New Hampshire	27.8	29.4	36.4	75.0	100.0
New Jersey	58.6	58.6	63.0	81.8	100.0
New Mexico	55.6	55.6	55.6	100.0	100.0
New York	54.2	54.6	58.4	81.4	100.0
North Carolina	41.5	41.5	52.9	92.9	100.0
North Dakota	33.3	33.3	75.0	100.0	100.0
Ohio	40.3	39.4	43.9	77.8	100.0
Oklahoma	37.5	37.5	52.9	80.0	100.0
Oregon	40.7	38.5	50.0	66.7	100.0
Pennsylvania	37.2	38.5	40.7	58.6	100.0
Puerto Rico	53.3	51.9	81.3	87.5	100.0
Rhode Island	40.0	40.0	44.4	60.0	100.0
South Carolina	32.4	33.3	42.9	57.1	100.0
South Dakota	35.7	35.7	41.7	100.0	100.0
Tennessee	31.9	30.2	42.9	73.3	100.0
Texas	54.3	57.0	61.3	83.3	100.0
Utah	71.4	71.4	66.7	100.0	100.0
Vermont	11.8	12.5	15.4	100.0	100.0
Virginia	47.9	50.0	67.7	100.0	100.0
Washington	54.2	54.2	57.1	80.0	100.0

Table 2.9 (continued)

State	All Degree Granting Institutions	All BA/BS Granting Institutions	All MA/MS Granting Institutions	All PhD Granting Institutions	All MD Granting Institutions
West Virginia	42.9	45.0	55.6	100.0	100.0
Wisconsin	55.6	55.9	60.0	71.4	100.0
Wyoming	100.0	100.0	100.0	100.0	na

NOTES: The units of multicampus universities and university systems were counted separately. See Appendix D for a complete list of the universities and colleges and their campuses in each state.

Calculating the percentage of institutions receiving federal R&D funding: For each state, the percentage of institutions receiving federal R&D funding was calculated for BA/BS, MA/MS, PhD, and MD degrees. The numerator was the sum of institutions granting a given degree that also received federal R&D funding; the denominator was the number of institutions granting a given degree. As a result, research institutions that do not grant degrees were not counted. Similarly, Regents and Board of Directors offices of the big university systems were not counted either.

INDIVIDUAL UNIVERSITIES AND COLLEGES: HOW DO THEY COMPARE IN OBTAINING FEDERAL R&D FUNDS?

Appendix D contains detailed information, by state, on the amount of federal funds that went to *every* four-year accredited university and college in the nation in FY 2002 for the conduct of R&D. Tables 2.10 and 2.11, both of which are presented here, and Tables C.1 through C.22 (see Appendix C) are based on the information in Appendix D. All of these tables identify the top-ranking universities and colleges in the nation on a variety of different dimensions likely to be of interest to anyone tracking federal R&D funds going to such institutions. Table C.23, the final table in Appendix C, is based not on the information in Appendix D but on additional information from the RaDiUS database. The contents of the one major "overview" table we provide here, Table 2.10, are discussed in detail below. A short discussion of Table 2.11 then follows, after which Tables C.1 through C.22 are briefly described.

Table 2.10 lists the 100 universities and colleges in the nation that received the most federal R&D funds in FY 2002, both including and excluding the federal R&D funds that went to medical schools. It shows that Johns Hopkins University ranked first in the nation in federal funds received for the conduct of R&D, regardless of whether the analysis included or excluded the federal R&D funds going to medical schools. Indeed, the success of Johns Hopkins University in winning federal R&D funds in FY 2002 so eclipsed that of other universities and colleges in the nation that the Medical School at Johns Hopkins University *alone* outranked all but nine of the universities and colleges in the nation in terms of the amount of federal R&D funds it garnered. In other words, if Johns Hopkins University Medical School *alone* (Table 2.11) is compared to all the universities and colleges *with* their medical schools (left side of Table 2.10), it ranks tenth. Furthermore, if Johns Hopkins University *without* its medical school (right side of Table 2.10) is compared to all the other universities and colleges *with* their medical schools (left side of Table 2.10), it still ranks first in the nation in federal R&D funds received. As noted previously, in the discussion of Tables 2.1 and 2.2, the presence of the Applied Physics Laboratory at Johns Hopkins University has much to do with the perennial top ranking of Johns Hopkins University with or with-

Table 2.10

Federal Funds Provided to Top 100 Universities and Colleges for Conduct of R&D in FY 2002 (Obligations in Millions)

Rank	University or College (Including Medical School)	Total Federal Funds Received for Conduct of R&D	Rank	University or College (Excluding Medical School)	Total Federal Funds Received for Conduct of R&D
1	Johns Hopkins University	968	1	Johns Hopkins University	604
2	University of Washington, Seattle	518	2	Massachusetts Institute of Technology	381
3	University of Pennsylvania	458	3	University of Washington, Seattle	267
4	University of Michigan, Ann Arbor	429	4	University of Wisconsin, Madison	253
5	University of California, Los Angeles	413	5	University of California, Berkeley	224
6	University of California, San Diego	406	6	University of California, San Diego	223
7	Stanford University	386	7	Pennsylvania State University, University Park	221
8	Massachusetts Institute of Technology	381	8	University of Michigan, Ann Arbor	216
9	University of Wisconsin, Madison	365	9	University of Illinois, Urbana-Champaign	206
10	Washington University, St Louis	360	10	University of Minnesota, Twin Cities	193
11	University of California, San Francisco	357	11	University of California, Los Angeles	193
12	University of Pittsburgh	337	12	Harvard University	193
13	Columbia University	335	13	Stanford University	178
14	Harvard University	333	14	University of Colorado, Boulder	157
15	Duke University	327	15	Cornell University	149
16	Yale University	312	16	University of Texas, Austin	141
17	University of Minnesota, Twin Cities	310	17	University of North Carolina, Chapel Hill	139
18	University of North Carolina, Chapel Hill	308	18	University of Texas, MD Anderson Cancer Center	137
19	Baylor College of Medicine	274	19	University of Maryland, College Park	135
20	University of Alabama, Birmingham	261	20	Columbia University	129
21	Cornell University	259	21	University of California, Davis	128
22	University of Southern California	224	22	University of Pittsburgh	120
23	University of California, Berkeley	224	23	University of Arizona	119
24	Vanderbilt University	224	24	University of Pennsylvania	118
25	Pennsylvania State University, University Park	221	25	University of Southern California	116
26	University of Illinois, Urbana-Champaign	206	26	University of Hawaii, Manoa	110
27	Case Western Reserve University	195	27	Ohio State University, Columbus (includes AES at Wooster)	110

Table 2.10 (continued)

Rank	University or College (Including Medical School)	Total Federal Funds Received for Conduct of R&D	Rank	University or College (Excluding Medical School)	Total Federal Funds Received for Conduct of R&D
28	University of Rochester	189	28	Georgia Institute of Technology	107
29	University of California, Davis	189	29	Rutgers University, New Brunswick	107
30	Emory University	189	30	University of Florida	102
31	University of Arizona	185	31	University of Alabama, Birmingham	101
32	University of Iowa	177	32	Texas A&M University, College Station	95
33	Boston University	176	33	Michigan State University	94
34	Ohio State University, Columbus (includes AES at Wooster)	173	34	Purdue University	93
35	University of Chicago	172	35	University of Georgia	91
36	University of Colorado System Health Sciences Center	171	36	Carnegie Mellon University	81
37	University of Virginia, Charlottesville	168	37	University of California, Irvine	81
38	Oregon Health & Science University	167	38	Duke University	81
39	University of Florida	165	39	Princeton University	80
40	University of Texas, Southwestern Medical Center at Dallas	163	40	Colorado State University	78
41	Northwestern University	161	41	University of Illinois, Chicago	78
42	University of Colorado, Boulder	157	42	Boston University	78
43	University of Utah	155	43	University of California, Santa Barbara	72
44	Mount Sinai School of Medicine	150	44	University of California, San Francisco	71
45	Mayo Medical School	148	45	Oregon State University	70
46	New York University	143	46	Rockefeller University	69
47	University of Illinois, Chicago	143	47	Northwestern University	69
48	University of Texas, Austin	141	48	University of Rochester	69
49	Yeshiva University	139	49	Yale University	67
50	University of Texas, MD Anderson Cancer Center	137	50	George Washington University (includes Mount Vernon campus)	66
51	University of California, Irvine	136	51	California Institute of Technology	64
52	University of Maryland, College Park	135	52	North Carolina State University	63
53	University of Maryland, Baltimore	128	53	University of Utah	60
54	University of Hawaii, Manoa	121	54	Iowa State University	60

Table 2.10 (continued)

Rank	University or College (Including Medical School)	Total Federal Funds Received for Conduct of R&D	Rank	University or College (Excluding Medical School)	Total Federal Funds Received for Conduct of R&D
55	University of Miami	120	55	Arizona State University, Tempe	57
56	University of Cincinnati	110	56	University of Indiana, Bloomington	56
57	Wake Forest University	109	57	University of Iowa	56
58	Georgia Institute of Technology	107	58	University of Massachusetts, Amherst	56
59	University of Medicine & Dentistry of New Jersey	107	59	Virginia Polytechnic Institute and State University	56
60	Rutgers University, New Brunswick	107	60	University of Missouri, Columbia	56
61	University of Kentucky	105	61	University of New Mexico	54
62	Wayne State University	103	62	University of Virginia, Charlottesville	54
63	University of Texas, Health Science Center at Houston	102	63	State University of New York, Stony Brook	53
64	Michigan State University	101	64	Utah State University	53
65	University of Connecticut	97	65	University of Alaska, Fairbanks	52
66	Indiana University—Purdue University at Indianapolis	96	66	University of Nebraska, Lincoln	52
67	Dartmouth College	95	67	University of Kentucky	51
68	Texas A&M University, College Station	95	68	Vanderbilt University	51
69	Purdue University	93	69	University of Tennessee, Knoxville	51
70	Medical University of South Carolina	92	70	Washington State University, Pullman	50
71	University of Massachusetts, Medical School at Worcester	92	71	State University of New York, Buffalo	50
72	University of Georgia	91	72	Case Western Reserve University	49
73	University of New Mexico	89	73	Emory University	49
74	State University of New York, Stony Brook	88	74	Oregon Health & Science University	49
75	Georgetown University	83	75	University of Chicago	48
76	George Washington University (includes Mount Vernon campus)	83	76	Wayne State University	47
77	Medical College of Wisconsin	82	77	University of Delaware	46
78	Carnegie Mellon University	81	78	University of Kansas, Lawrence	46
79	University of Texas, Health Science Center at San Antonio	81	79	Louisiana State University, Baton Rouge	45
80	University of Texas, Medical Branch-Galveston	81	80	Washington University, St Louis	45
81	Thomas Jefferson University	80	81	University of Connecticut	44
82	Princeton University	80	82	Mississippi State University	44

Table 2.10 (continued)

Rank	University or College (Including Medical School)	Total Federal Funds Received for Conduct of R&D	Rank	University or College (Excluding Medical School)	Total Federal Funds Received for Conduct of R&D
83	Virginia Commonwealth University	79	83	University of South Florida, Tampa	43
84	Colorado State University	78	84	University of Miami	41
85	Brown University	75	85	Brown University	40
86	State University of New York, Buffalo	74	86	University of Oregon	40
87	University of South Florida, Tampa	72	87	University of New Hampshire, Durham	38
88	University of Vermont	72	88	Florida State University	37
89	University of California, Santa Barbara	72	89	New York University	36
90	Oregon State University	70	90	University of California, Santa Cruz	36
91	Rockefeller University	69	91	University of Notre Dame	35
92	University of Missouri, Columbia	67	92	Tulane University	35
93	California Institute of Technology	64	93	University of Maryland, Baltimore County	35
94	North Carolina State University	63	94	Dartmouth College	34
95	Iowa State University	60	95	University of California, Riverside	34
96	Tulane University	60	96	Georgetown University	34
97	Arizona State University, Tempe	57	97	Montana State University, Bozeman	33
98	University of Indiana, Bloomington	56	98	West Virginia University	33
99	Tufts University	56	99	University of Maryland, Baltimore	32
100	University of Massachusetts, Amherst	56	100	University of South Carolina, Columbia	32

NOTE: See Table C.10 in Appendix C for more detailed information.

out its medical school. For example, in FY 2002, the Applied Physics Laboratory received almost 50 percent more federal funds with which to conduct R&D than did the remainder of the non-medical-school portion of Johns Hopkins University.

Similarly, the Massachusetts Institute of Technology, which does not have a medical school, received more federal R&D funds than did all but seven universities that do have medical schools. That is, in the national ranking that included *all* the federal funds going to institutions of higher education for the conduct of R&D in FY 2002, the Massachusetts Institute of Technology ranked below the universities of Washington at Seattle, Pennsylvania, Michigan at Ann Arbor, California at Los Angeles, and California at San Diego, and Stanford University *only* because the R&D funds going to the medical schools at these universities were included in their totals.

Several other institutions of higher education also frequented the top ten ranks of U.S. universities and colleges receiving federal R&D funds in FY 2002, regardless of whether the federal R&D funds going to medical schools were included or excluded. Foremost among these was the University of Washington at Seattle, which ranked second in the nation when federal R&D funds going to medical schools were included and third when they were excluded. Similarly, the University of Michigan at Ann Arbor ranked fourth in the nation when these funds were included and eighth when they were excluded; the University of Wisconsin at Madison ranked ninth with them included and fourth with them excluded; and the University of California at San Diego ranked sixth with them both included *and* excluded.

When we expanded the ranks to encompass the top 20 universities and colleges in the nation, Stanford University ranked seventh when federal R&D funds going to medical schools were included and thirteenth when they were excluded. Columbia University ranked thirteenth with them included and twentieth with them excluded; Harvard University ranked fourteenth with them and twelfth without them; the University of Minnesota in the Twin Cities ranked seventeenth with them and tenth without them; and, finally, the University of North Carolina at Chapel Hill ranked eighteenth with them and seventeenth without them.

In summary, 12 universities and colleges receiving federal R&D funds in FY 2002 ranked in the top 20, regardless of whether the analysis included or excluded the R&D funds going to medical schools. Similarly, 80 institutions of higher education ranked among the top 100 in FY 2002, regardless of whether the medical school funds were included or not. Such numbers strongly suggest that federally supported R&D activities are concentrated in only a few of the nation's many universities and colleges. Indeed, totaling the federal R&D funds going to these 80 universities and colleges in FY 2002 revealed that they received 71 percent of all federal funds awarded to universities and colleges for the conduct of R&D in FY 2002. Hence, it is clear that, while many of the nation's universities and colleges received some federal R&D funds in FY 2002, the majority of federally supported R&D activities were highly concentrated in only a few of them.

Table 2.11 shows that there was a similar concentration of federal R&D funds among the nation's medical schools in FY 2002. Specifically, the top ten medical schools listed in the table received 29 percent of all federal R&D funds awarded to medical schools in FY 2002. When the top 20 medical schools are looked at, the percentage of all federal R&D funds awarded to these medical schools in FY 2002 increases to 47 percent. In short, in FY 2002, while all but one medical school in the nation received some federal R&D funds, a mere 16 percent of medical schools received almost 50 percent of all federal funds provided to such institutions for the conduct of R&D.

Table 2.11

Federal Funds Provided to Medical Schools for Conduct of R&D in FY 2002, by Medical School in Rank Order (Obligations)

Rank	Medical School[a]	Total Federal Funds Received for Conduct of R&D
1	John Hopkins University School of Medicine	364,493,858
2	University of Pennsylvania School of Medicine	340,142,057
3	Washington University School of Medicine	315,794,675
4	University of California, San Francisco—School of Medicine	285,432,106
5	Baylor College of Medicine	272,426,074
6	University of Washington School of Medicine	250,935,417
7	Duke University School of Medicine	246,734,592
8	Yale University School of Medicine	245,736,787
9	University of California, Los Angeles—Geffen School of Medicine	219,581,899
10	University of Pittsburgh School of Medicine	217,120,867
11	University of Michigan Medical School	213,169,712
12	Stanford University School of Medicine	207,983,087
13	Columbia University College of Physicians and Surgeons	206,221,353
14	University of California, San Diego—School of Medicine	182,427,601
15	Vanderbilt University School of Medicine	172,685,765
16	University of North Carolina at Chapel Hill School of Medicine	168,763,891
17	University of Texas, Southwestern Medical Center at Dallas	162,430,979
18	University of Alabama School of Medicine	159,576,895
19	University of Colorado System Health Sciences Center	158,631,658
20	Mount Sinai School of Medicine	148,321,247
21	Mayo Medical School	148,057,109
22	Case Western Reserve University School of Medicine	146,221,297
23	Emory University School of Medicine	140,494,101
24	Harvard Medical School	139,790,964
25	Yeshiva University Albert Einstein College of Medicine	129,827,962
26	University of Chicago Pritzker School of Medicine	124,946,536
27	University of Rochester School of Medicine	120,787,707
28	University of Iowa College of Medicine	120,338,303
29	Oregon Health and Science University School of Medicine	118,142,774
30	University of Minnesota School of Medicine—Twin Cities	116,598,707

Table 2.11 (continued)

Rank	Medical School[a]	Total Federal Funds Received for Conduct of R&D
31	University of Virginia School of Medicine	113,855,400
32	University of Wisconsin School of Medicine	112,443,954
33	Cornell University—Weill Medical College	109,559,176
34	University of Southern California Keck School of Medicine	107,512,986
35	New York University School of Medicine	106,717,559
36	Wake Forest University School of Medicine	103,314,301
37	Boston University School of Medicine	97,938,833
38	University of Maryland School of Medicine	96,112,532
39	University of Utah School of Medicine	94,336,624
40	Northwestern University, Chicago—Medical Center	92,415,757
41	University of Massachusetts, Medical School at Worcester	89,185,560
42	Indiana University School of Medicine at Indianapolis	88,137,186
43	Medical University of South Carolina	85,323,004
44	University of Cincinnati College of Medicine	84,025,831
45	Medical College of Wisconsin	80,151,361
46	Thomas Jefferson University—Jefferson Medical College	80,137,024
47	University of Miami School of Medicine	78,516,005
48	University of Texas, Medical Branch-Galveston	78,144,249
49	University of Texas, Health Science Center at Houston	77,354,824
50	University of Texas, Health Science Center at San Antonio	70,927,736
51	University of Arizona College of Medicine	65,563,658
52	University of Illinois at Chicago College of Medicine	64,936,955
53	Ohio State University College of Medicine and Public Health	63,661,780
54	University of Florida College of Medicine	62,635,081
55	University of California, Davis—School of Medicine	60,774,529
56	Dartmouth Medical School	60,774,511
57	UMDNJ—Robert Wood Johnson Medical School	57,610,612
58	Wayne State University School of Medicine	56,012,576
59	University of Vermont College of Medicine	55,148,661
60	University of California, Irvine—School of Medicine	54,424,609
61	University of Kentucky College of Medicine	53,986,489
62	University of Connecticut Health Center	52,807,496
63	Virginia Commonwealth University—Medical College of Virginia	52,359,055
64	Georgetown University Medical School	49,236,886
65	Rush University Medical College	46,929,666
66	UMDNJ—New Jersey Medical School	46,058,128
67	Tufts University School of Medicine	42,902,847
68	Pennsylvania State University College of Medicine	41,218,351
69	University of Arkansas—Medical Sciences	40,106,026
70	University of Tennessee System Health Science Center at Memphis	36,888,853
71	University of Kansas Medical Center	36,588,814
72	Brown University Medical School	35,250,077

Table 2.11 (continued)

Rank	Medical School[a]	Total Federal Funds Received for Conduct of R&D
73	University of New Mexico Health Science Center	34,270,183
74	State University of New York—Stony Brook Health Science Center	34,156,594
75	University of Oklahoma Health Sciences Center	32,103,443
76	Morehouse School of Medicine	29,200,036
77	Temple University School of Medicine	28,869,370
78	University of South Florida College of Medicine	28,743,812
79	University of Nebraska System Medical Center	28,145,257
80	University of Puerto Rico School of Medicine	27,693,231
81	University of Louisville School of Medicine	27,405,491
82	Medical College of Georgia	25,405,660
83	Loyola University Chicago Stritch School of Medicine	25,096,368
84	State University of New York—Health Science Center at Brooklyn	24,961,414
85	Tulane University School of Medicine	24,433,394
86	State University of New York—Buffalo School of Medicine & Biomedical Sciences	24,305,822
87	Saint Louis University School of Medicine	22,777,885
88	Meharry Medical College	21,981,183
89	Louisiana State University School of Medicine at New Orleans	20,700,295
90	New York Medical College	20,157,677
91	Charles R. Drew University of Medicine and Science	16,990,406
92	George Washington University School of Medicine and Health Sciences	16,494,785
93	Howard University College of Medicine	16,004,542
94	State University of New York—Health Science Center at Syracuse	15,970,579
95	Drexel University—Health Sciences	15,610,040
96	University of Mississippi Medical Center	14,223,773
97	Texas A&M University Health Science Center	13,922,263
98	Loma Linda University School of Medicine	13,200,505
99	University of Missouri at Columbia School of Medicine	11,798,199
100	University of Nevada School of Medicine	11,720,921
101	Medical College of Ohio	11,562,036
102	University of South Alabama College of Medicine	11,153,321
103	West Virginia University School of Medicine	10,646,187
104	Louisiana State University School of Medicine at Shreveport	10,535,566
105	University of Hawaii School of Medicine	10,418,793
106	Albany Medical College	10,113,727
107	Texas Tech University Health Sciences Center	8,381,658
108	University of North Dakota School of Medicine and Health Sciences	8,012,392
109	Wright State University School of Medicine	7,969,505
110	Michigan State University College of Human Medicine	7,336,003
111	University of South Dakota School of Medicine	6,877,606
112	Universidad Central del Caribe School of Medicine	6,666,018

Table 2.11 (continued)

Rank	Medical School[a]	Total Federal Funds Received for Conduct of R&D
113	Ponce School of Medicine	6,077,903
114	University of Missouri at Kansas City School of Medicine	6,059,137
115	Eastern Virginia Medical School—Medical College of Hampton Roads	5,956,505
116	Finch University of Health Sciences—The Chicago Medical School	5,903,512
118	East Carolina University Brody School of Medicine	3,544,209
119	Creighton University School of Medicine	3,531,708
120	University of South Carolina School of Medicine	3,248,573
121	Marshall University John C. Edwards School of Medicine	2,581,852
122	East Tennessee State University College of Medicine	2,541,027
123	University of Minnesota School of Medicine at Duluth	1,952,299
124	Northeastern Ohio Universities College of Medicine	1,380,226
125	Mercer University School of Medicine	1,324,462
126	The Uniformed Services University of the Health Sciences	0

[a] Osteopathic, chiropractic, and podiatry schools not included.

OTHER CUTS THROUGH THE DATA

The ways in which one can use the information in this report to look at the distribution of federal R&D funds among the nation's universities and colleges are virtually endless. Tables C.1 through C. 22 in Appendix C present the most common of these views.

Tables C.11 through C.16 show the top 50 universities and colleges, including and excluding medical schools, that received R&D funds from, respectively, HHS, NSF, DOD, NASA, DOE, and USDA. Note that each of these tables includes details on how these federal R&D funds were conveyed to the institutions—i.e., via contracts, grants, or other mechanisms. Tables C.17 and C.18 provide details on the top 50 public and top 50 private universities and colleges that received federal R&D funds. The information in Table C.17 includes the federal R&D funds going to medical schools; that in Table C.18 excludes those funds. National averages are provided at the top of these two tables.

Tables C.19 and C.20 provide comparable information for land-grant and non-land-grant universities and colleges; Tables C.21 and C.22 do the same for historically black colleges and universities (HBCUs) and non-HBCUs. The first set, Tables C.19 and C.20, shows that the top individual land-grant institutions received far fewer federal R&D dollars in FY 2002 than their non-land-grant institution counterparts did. However, these two tables also show that the *average* land-grant institution received at least three times more federal R&D funds in FY 2002 than the *average* non-land-grant institution did. Similarly, Tables C.21 and C.22 show that the top individual HBCUs received far fewer federal R&D dollars in FY 2002 than their non-HBCU counterparts did. But unlike the situation with land-grant and non-land-grant institutions, the *average* HBCU did not receive more federal R&D funds in FY 2002 than the *average* non-HBCU did. Indeed, the *average* HBCU received substantially less than one-quarter of the federal R&D dollars that the *average* non-HBCU received. Viewed another way, the top recipient of federal R&D dollars among land-grant institutions in FY 2002 ranked ninth among the non-land-grant institutions when medical schools were included and fourth when medical schools were excluded. In contrast, the top recipient of federal R&D dollars among HBCUs in FY 2002 ranked 121st among non-HBCUs when medical schools were included and 126th when medical schools were excluded.

Chapter Three

CONCLUSIONS AND IMPLICATIONS

CONCLUSIONS

Our analysis found that, between 1996 and 2002, total federal R&D funds going to universities and colleges grew from $12.8 billion to $21.4 billion, for an overall increase of 45.7 percent in constant 1996 dollars. To put this growth in perspective, the increase in federal R&D funds going to universities and colleges between FY 1996 and FY 2002 was more than double the overall increase in federal R&D funds going to *all* performers for the conduct of R&D in constant 1996 dollars (i.e., 45.7 percent versus 20.9 percent).

Sizable increases in funding to HHS (specifically for the National Institutes of Health) accounted for a substantial portion of this growth. The main recipients of these funds were medical schools. In FY 2002, 45 percent of all federal R&D funds that went to universities and colleges went directly to the internal units of these institutions that make up their medical schools. Because some states have no medical schools and other states have many, the distribution of federal R&D funds going to the universities and colleges in the various states is thus considerably skewed.

IMPLICATIONS FOR FEDERAL R&D PRIORITIES

The profile of federally funded R&D at universities and colleges that emerges from this analysis raises issues of proportionality. Specifically, in the current funding profile, approximately two-thirds of the federal funds going to universities and colleges for the conduct of R&D focus on only one field of science—life science—and federal R&D funding is concentrated at only a few research universities.[1] These facts raise the following questions:

- Are biomedical and health care issues so clearly at the top of the nation's agenda that they merit two-thirds of all federal funds provided to universities and colleges for the conduct of R&D?

- Are other critical national needs that have substantial R&D components (such as environment, energy, homeland security, and education) getting the attention they require?

_____

[1] Eiseman, Koizumi, and Fossum, 2002, pp. 21–32.

- Are science and engineering students at universities and colleges that do not receive a notable share of federal R&D funds receiving a lower-quality education? Are their career opportunities hampered as a result?

IMPLICATIONS FOR DECISIONMAKING

The information on federal R&D funds going to the nation's universities and colleges can vary significantly, depending on the source of the data and how the data were collected. By taking a new approach to gathering data on the federal R&D funds going to universities and colleges, this analysis has endeavored to change the dialogue in this area, shifting it from a dialogue focused on the accuracy of numbers to a dialogue focused on federal policies.

This analysis provides information that should help clarify three important issues for university and college decisionmakers as well as federal agencies.

First, universities and colleges lack long-term, consistent data with which to gauge their success at acquiring R&D funding. In the absence of such data, credible comparisons among institutions cannot be made. This analysis enables all universities and colleges with R&D activity to know where they stand relative to other institutions in their ability to obtain federal R&D funds.

Second, the significance of how the federal R&D funds are conveyed to the universities and colleges (i.e., grant versus contract) should now be clearer. That is, this analysis disproves the persistent stereotype that *all* federal R&D funds are conveyed to universities and colleges via peer-reviewed project grants. As a result, all universities and colleges now have accurate information on the funding mechanisms the federal government has actually used to transmit R&D funds to them, so they can better assess the rights they have to any intellectual property resulting from such R&D.

Third, federal R&D agencies now have the information needed to better coordinate and set policy for their R&D "boot-strap" programs, such as EPSCoR, among themselves. That is, armed with the data in this report, federal R&D agencies can now specifically target all universities and colleges in the nation that truly need federal assistance to build their R&D capacity.

OTHER IMPLICATIONS

And finally, Walshok et al. suggest the growing importance of the connection between the amount of federal R&D funds going to universities and colleges and the general economy of the region in which these institutions are located.[2] For example, as noted in Chapter One, many universities and colleges are the major employers in a number of cities across the nation. And cities have found that the research their local universities are conducting—most of which is funded by the federal government— has tremendous economic value when it is actively shaped and fostered by skilled

---

[2] Walshok, Furtek, Lee, and Windham, 2002, pp. 27–42.

innovators and entrepreneurs. To cite one example, San Diego made effective use of local university research in successfully restructuring the economy of the city and the region.[3] This topic merits further exploration, given the evidence that the nation's universities and colleges are vital assets upon which the R&D investment decisions of individual federal agencies have a tremendous influence.

---

[3] Walshok, Furtek, Lee, and Windham, 2002, pp. 27–42.

THE RaDiUS DATABASE

The information on federal research and development (R&D) presented in this report comes from the RaDiUS (Research and Development in the United States) database. The RAND Corporation created RaDiUS, in cooperation with the National Science Foundation (NSF), to track, at both the aggregate and the detailed level, all the activities that are supported each fiscal year with the funds officially reported as paying for (i.e., purchasing) the "conduct of R&D" in the Budget of the U.S. Government. As such, RaDiUS does not attempt to independently define which federally supported activities do and do not constitute R&D. Instead, RaDiUS starts with the baseline of federal R&D funding that is presented annually in the federal budget and systematically follows all dollars officially designated as "conduct of R&D" dollars through the federal bureaucracy's many layers to where they are actually spent—i.e., RaDiUS tracks the transformation of federal R&D Budget Authority into federal R&D Obligations. By taking this approach, RaDiUS effectively defines R&D as the activities on which federal dollars that have been officially designated as R&D dollars are spent.

This approach allows one to distinguish between federally funded activities that are officially designated as R&D activities and those that are seen as non-R&D activities. Specifically, even though all federally supported R&D activities involve the study and analysis of various subjects or phenomena, the federal government sees "R&D" and "studies and analyses" as two mutually exclusive categories and therefore tracks them separately. While the dividing line between these two categories may seem blurry to many, federal procurement officials decide which activities fall into which category on a daily basis. In FY 2002, these officials determined that 40,251 of the contracts that the federal government had awarded were R&D because they involved

> increasing knowledge in science; applying increased scientific knowledge or exploiting the potential of scientific discoveries and improvements in technology to advance the state of art; and[/or] systematically using increases in scientific knowledge and advances in state of art to design, develop, test, or evaluate new products or services. (Federal Procurement Report 2002.)

In contrast, these same officials determined that 8,714 of the contracts that had been awarded involved "studies and analyses" rather than R&D, because they were "orga–nized, analytic assessments that provide insights for understanding complex issues or improving policy development or decision making" (Federal Procurement Report 2002).

As a consequence, the 40,251 federal contracts designated as R&D are contained in RaDiUS and therefore were part of this analysis, whereas the 8,714 contracts designated as studies and analyses are not. To put this in the specific context of institutions of higher education, the federal government made a total of 117,517 R&D awards to the nation's universities and colleges in FY 2002. Of these, 108,119 were grants (10,516 being formula grants), 6,817 were cooperative agreements, and 2,581 were contracts. In contrast, the same universities and colleges received a total of 235 federal contracts for the conduct of "studies and analyses" in FY 2002.

The use of the terms *science* and *technology* in the context of the federal government can also be a source of confusion when defining federal R&D activities. The confusion in this case flows from the fact that the federal government uses *science* and *technology* to describe the functional missions, in whole or part, of three—but only three—of the 24 federal agencies that fund R&D activities every year. Specifically, all of the funds controlled by the National Science Foundation and part of the funds controlled by the National Aeronautics and Space Administration and the Department of Energy are characterized, for federal budgeting purposes, as supporting "General Science, Space, and Technology" activities (Functional Classification 250, OMB Circular A-11, Exhibit 79B). However, only a portion of the "General Science, Space, and Technology" funds each of these agencies spends is actually for "R&D" activities.

Consequently, when discussing this particular aspect of the federal budget, great care must be taken not to view *R&D* and *science and technology* as synonymous. Indeed, to minimize the confusion between these terms, OMB does not use *science* or *technology* to define "R&D" in its instructions to federal agencies regarding annual budget requests (OMB Circular A-11, Section 84 and Exhibit 79B). In recent years, however, OMB has prepared a special analysis of the "Federal Science and Technology (FS&T) Budget" that encompasses "nearly all of federal basic research, over 80 percent of federal applied research, and about half of civilian development" in an effort to facilitate the tracking of research and nondefense development through the budget and appropriations process (Budget of the U.S. Government, Analytical Perspectives). Use of the terms *science* and *technology* in the context of the FS&T Budget, however, is not parallel to that in the functional categories of the budget; and, in turn, neither use of *science* and *technology* equates to the term *R&D* as used in the context of the federal budget.

To follow the R&D dollars as they flow through the federal bureaucracy, RaDiUS draws on the data that the government's budget, transaction, and general tracking systems already collect and weaves the data together to form a complete picture of federal R&D funding from its most aggregate to its most detailed level. Because 75 percent of all federal R&D dollars that descend through the rungs of the federal bureaucracy and are ultimately spent by federal agencies (i.e., obligated) leave the federal government in the form of contracts, grants, and cooperative agreements, the vast majority of information in the most detailed level of RaDiUS comes from two sources: the Federal Procurement Data System (FPDS), which tracks all federal contracts, and the Federal Assistance Awards Data System (FAADS), which tracks all federal grants and cooperative agreements.

The Federal Procurement Data Center (FPDC), a unit of the U.S. General Services Administration (GSA), maintains and operates the FPDS. FPDC was created by the Office of Federal Procurement Policy Act in 1974 (PL 93-400), which mandated that the Administrator of the Office of Federal Procurement Policy "establish an automated system for collecting, evaluating, and disseminating information about Federal procurement contracts" to facilitate federal planning, analysis, and general program evaluation. Housed initially inside the Department of Defense, the FPDC began collecting information in 1979 on all contracts the federal government awards. All this information was to be placed in FPDS. In 1982, FPDC and the FPDS were moved to GSA, where they remain today. The FPDS contains summary information on all contracts awarded by federal agencies with a value of less than $25,000 (i.e., small purchases) and detailed information on all contracts awarded by federal agencies with a value of over $25,000 (i.e., large contracts). Among the details collected about every large contract in the FPDS is the "purpose" of the contract, so the data elements in the FPDS tell whether the purpose of the contract was to obtain airplanes, electricity, training, etc., or to conduct R&D. These determinations are made by the procurement officers in each federal agency, who, being directly involved in negotiating the terms and conditions of the contract, are uniquely situated to know the specific purpose for which a contract is awarded (i.e., whether it is for R&D or something else). Hence, by using the FPDS, one can identify every R&D contract the federal government has awarded and determine who is conducting the R&D, where they are conducting it, and how much they are authorized to spend on it.

The FAADS is the FPDS's counterpart in that it collects detailed information on all "nonprocurement" awards made by the federal government—i.e., on all grants and cooperative agreements (as well as on loans, direct payments, etc.) made by any federal agency. The FAADS is authorized by Titles 13 and 31 of the U.S. Code, as well as an OMB special designation, and is operated and maintained by the Census Bureau in the Department of Commerce. Pursuant to this authority, federal agencies must provide detailed information to the Census Bureau on virtually every financial assistance award (i.e., nonprocurement award) made to a nonfederal party and have done so quarterly since 1982. In turn, the Census Bureau makes this information available to Congress and the general public for use in planning, analysis, and program evaluation. Among the details the system collects on each financial assistance award are the federal program making the award, the name and location of the award recipient, and the amount of the assistance award. Information is also collected on the type of entity receiving the award (e.g., state-controlled institution of higher education, privately controlled institution of higher education), as well as on the type of the assistance provided to the entity (e.g., project grant, formula grant, cooperative agreement). Because the FAADS does not directly collect information on which assistance awards involve the conduct of R&D, it has been critically important to the creation and maintenance of RaDiUS that every award contained in the FAADS is directly linked to one of the programs listed in the Catalog of Federal Domestic Assistance (CFDA), which does indicate which federal programs involve the conduct of R&D.

The CFDA is a compendium of all the programs, projects, services, and other types of assistance provided to nonfederal entities by all agencies of the federal government. It was created by the Federal Program Information Act (PL 95-220) in 1977, which required OMB "to establish and maintain a computerized program information system which is capable of identifying all existing Federal domestic assistance programs." PL 98-169 transferred the operational responsibilities for the CFDA from OMB to GSA, which has maintained it since 1984. GSA updates the CFDA every year, with the assistance of OMB, so that parties interested in learning about any type of assistance (both financial and nonfinancial) offered by the federal government need to consult just this one source to find out about all such assistance available. Each CFDA listing contains a detailed description of the purpose or objective of the federal program, the type of assistance the program provides, the program's eligibility requirements, and how to apply for the assistance. These listings also indicate which federal agency is providing the assistance and the budget or treasury account from which any program funds come. The CFDA includes all federal programs that provide grants or cooperative agreements to support R&D activities, and the program descriptions state whether or not they support R&D. Consequently, one can identify the R&D grants and cooperative agreements that federal programs have awarded by connecting the CFDA numbers carried on the individual awards in the FAADS to the programs listed in the CFDA that have R&D as their stated objective. For example, all the FAADS awards carrying the CFDA number 10.219 involve R&D, because the stated objective of the CFDA Program 10.219 is "to carry out research focused on environmental effects of biotechnology."

The R&D information pulled from the FPDS, FAADS, and CFDA is the most accurate and reliable such information available, because all three of these official federal data systems are closely monitored, regularly updated, and promptly corrected when errors are discovered. Such is also the case with the data in RaDiUS that are pulled directly from the MAX Budget Information System, which is the Executive Office of the President's data system for collecting, validating, analyzing, and publishing the Budget of the U. S. Government (i.e., the President's Budget). The data from the MAX Budget Information System is the official source of information on how many federal dollars are allocated each fiscal year to support the conduct of R&D, and hence it is the funding baseline on which RaDiUS is built. In short, RaDiUS pulls data from the MAX Budget Information System, FPDS, FAADS, and CFDA, and augments these data with data from many other, smaller information collections scattered throughout the federal government. RaDiUS then systematically weaves all these data together using Treasury Account numbers, Federal Information Processing Standards (FIPS) codes, award numbers, and/or comparable identifying codes carried on each individual record to create a complete picture of the R&D work being conducted with the support of federal funds. The entities that actually conduct this federally supported R&D include federal laboratories, national laboratories, nonprofit organizations, for-profit corporations, and the nation's universities and colleges.

METHODOLOGY

Because our primary focus in the analysis covered by this report was on the federal research and development (R&D) awards that go to the nation's universities and colleges, we created a subset of the RaDiUS (Research and Development in the United States) database records that contained only the federal R&D awards made to four-year accredited public and private U.S. universities and colleges. This "extract file" included every permutation of every variation of every name under which a university or college might be conducting business with the federal government. To ease data handling and facilitate our analysis, we electronically separated the "extract file" into 52 spreadsheets—one for each of the 50 states, the District of Columbia, and Puerto Rico. We then manually checked each spreadsheet to ensure that all entities identified as universities or colleges in the records were indeed such institutions and, most important, to "normalize" (i.e., standardize) their names. The latter process took several months to complete, because it was very common to find that a single university or college appeared in the assembled records under a variety of names.

Please note that the federal funds universities received to manage and operate federally funded R&D centers (FFRDCs) are *not* included in this report. Specifically, the funds excluded from this report are those the California Institute of Technology received for the Jet Propulsion Laboratory; those Stanford University received for the Linear Accelerator Center; those the University of California received for Lawrence Berkeley, Lawrence Livermore, and Los Alamos National Laboratories; those the University of Chicago received for Argonne National Laboratory; those Iowa State University received for Ames Laboratory; those the Massachusetts Institute of Technology received for Lincoln Laboratory; those Princeton University received for the Plasma Physics Laboratory; those Cornell University received for the National Astronomy and Ionosphere Center; and those Carnegie Mellon University received for the Software Engineering Institute. While all these laboratories annually receive substantial amounts of federal R&D funds, they are not legally a part of the universities that manage and operate them. Instead, the federal government owns all these laboratories. As a consequence, no federal R&D funds that these laboratories receive are credited to the universities that manage and operate them.

The amount of data that needed to be prepared for analysis was substantial. Specifically, we wanted to present information on the total federal funds going to universities and colleges in the 50 states, the District of Columbia, and Puerto Rico for the conduct of R&D for a number of fiscal years to reveal overall trends. We also wanted to take a detailed, in-depth look at the internal dynamics of the federal R&D funding process for one fiscal year (i.e., FY 2002) to identify how every individual university and college within the 50 states, the District of Columbia, and Puerto Rico fared in the competition for federal funds with which to conduct R&D. To do this, the universe of like institutions was identified for every type of university and college that was found to be receiving federal R&D funds. For example, when it was discovered that one college of chiropractic medicine received federal R&D funds, all accredited colleges of chiropractic medicine were identified and added to the list of higher education institutions that were eligible to receive federal R&D funds (see Appendix D for a complete list of these institutions). The colleges of osteopathic medicine and optometry were treated similarly. Because no school of podiatry receives federal R&D funds, the list of eligible institutions contained in Appendix D does not include these schools. Please note that one school that does indeed grant a degree in podiatry is included in this report, however, because it also grants degrees in several other fields of study that routinely receive federal R&D funds. The sole exception to this general rule of inclusion involves colleges of Oriental medicine. When we found that one school of Oriental medicine was receiving federal R&D funds, we also discovered that there is no identifiable universe of such institutions in the United States; therefore, this report includes only one institution of this type.

In addition, we identified a number of potentially important characteristics of individual universities and colleges and tied them directly to each individual institution. For example, to determine whether public universities and colleges fare differently from private universities and colleges in their bids for federal R&D funds, we individually identified all four-year accredited public and private universities and colleges in the nation and specifically "tagged" their R&D awards in the data set. Similar steps also tagged federal R&D awards going to land-grant universities and colleges and Historically Black Colleges and Universities (HBCUs), since these are the other dimensions that reports on federal R&D funding for academic institutions commonly note. All this was in addition to manually checking that the awards that went to multicampus universities were attributed to the correct campuses. The latter activity went more smoothly than anticipated because, for most multicampus institutions, the specific campus receiving the federal funds was indeed noted. In a few instances, however, it was necessary to contact the institution directly to verify which component campuses had received which federal R&D awards.

By far the most complicated part of preparing the data for this analysis was identifying all the awards that went to medical schools. This distinction is of critical importance for this analysis for two reasons. First, from the outset of this study, we suspected that a substantial amount of the federal R&D funds traditionally viewed as going generally to universities and colleges actually went to the medical schools within these institutions. Second, while 126 accredited medical schools are affiliated with the nation's universities and colleges, these schools are not evenly distributed among the states. Specifically, the states of New York, California, Texas, and Illinois are home to 12, 9, 7, and 7 medical schools, respectively; the states of Arizona, Colorado, Hawaii, Indiana, Iowa, Kansas, Mississippi, Nevada, New Hampshire, New Mexico, North Dakota, Oklahoma, Oregon, Rhode Island, Utah, and Vermont have only one medical school each; and the states of Alaska, Delaware, Idaho, Maine,

Montana, and Wyoming have none. Consequently, to be fair to the last group of states, it was critical to be able to determine the precise effects that the presence of a medical school(s) had on the overall ability of a state's universities and colleges to acquire federal R&D funds. So, to facilitate this analysis, it was necessary to take great care to "tag" accurately all individual federal R&D awards that went to all medical schools. Because the vast majority of federal R&D funds going to medical schools come from NIH, a special data file from NIH that identified all of the awards that it made to medical schools in FY 2002 was of tremendous help in this endeavor.

The one additional noteworthy adjustment we made to the data for this analysis was to change the characterization of the grants made pursuant to CFDA Program 10.216 from "project grants" to "formula grants." While this change affected only a handful of the many thousands of R&D awards analyzed in this study, it was important because the R&D grants awarded under CFDA Program 10.216 were available to only 18 universities and colleges in the entire nation, which were the same institutions that received "formula grants" under a companion CFDA program operated by the Department of Agriculture (i.e., CFDA Program 10.205). Ideally, this change would have ensured that all the awards described as "project grants" in this analysis had been awarded pursuant to a peer-review process. Such is not the case, however, because a number of the project grants contained in RaDiUS and included in this report were congressional earmarks. That is, they were special allocations of federal R&D funds that Congress made to specific universities and colleges without the benefit of an impartial assessment of the scientific merits of the R&D to be conducted and without consideration of whether the university or college receiving the funds was actually the institution best able to conduct the R&D.

In FY 2002, congressional earmarks of federal R&D funds for universities and colleges totaled $1.8 billion (Chronicle of Higher Education, 9/27/02). Had all of these earmarks involved the conduct of R&D, they would have constituted 8.4 percent of all the federal R&D funds showcased in this report. However, a substantial amount of them were for constructing R&D facilities or acquiring major R&D equipment, neither of which are tracked in RaDiUS or analyzed in this study. A review of the individual earmarks that involve the conduct of R&D, as opposed to the construction of R&D facilities or the acquisition of major R&D equipment, indicates that between 6 and 7 percent of the R&D funds included in RaDiUS and this study involve congressional earmarks. While at least some of the R&D awards that all major R&D agencies make annually are congressional earmarks, none of the resulting grants that move these funds to their designated recipients is specifically "tagged" in agency data systems as being an earmark. As a result, individual earmarks cannot be systematically identified and, therefore, are not separately analyzed in this report.

ADDITIONAL TABLES

The following tables appear on the CD-ROM attached to the back cover of this report:

Table C.1 (Detail)—Federal Funds for Conduct of R&D Provided in FY 1996–2002 to Universities and Colleges, Including Medical Schools, by State in Rank Order

Table C.2 (Detail)—States Ranked According to Total Federal Funds Received for Conduct of R&D in FY 2002 by Their Resident Universities and Colleges, Including and Excluding Medical Schools

Table C.3 (Detail)—Agencies Providing Federal Funds for Conduct of R&D in FY 2002 to Universities and Colleges, Including Medical Schools, by State

Table C.4 (Detail)—Agencies Providing Federal Funds for Conduct of R&D in FY 2002 to Universities and Colleges, Excluding Medical Schools, by State

Table C.5 (Detail)—Agencies Providing Federal Funds for Conduct of R&D in FY 2002 to Universities and Colleges, Excluding Medical Schools, by State (with highlights)

Table C.6 (Detail)—Federal Funds for Conduct of R&D Provided in FY 2002 to Universities and Colleges, Including Medical Schools, by State in Rank Order

Table C.7 (Detail)—Federal Funds for Conduct of R&D Provided in FY 2002 to Universities and Colleges, Excluding Medical Schools, by State in Rank Order

Table C.8 (Detail)—Number of Universities and Colleges Receiving Federal Funds for Conduct of R&D in FY 2002, by State and by Types of Degrees Granted by Universities and Colleges Located in State

Table C.9 (Detail)—Top 100 Universities and Colleges, Including and Excluding Medical Schools, Provided Federal Funds in FY 2002 for Conduct of R&D

Table C.10 (Detail)—Federal Funds Provided to Medical Schools for Conduct of R&D in FY 2002, by Medical School in Rank Order

Table C.11—Top 50 Universities and Colleges, Including and Excluding Medical Schools, Provided Funds by Department of Health and Human Services in FY 2002 for Conduct of R&D

This appendix provides a separate table for each state, in alphabetical order, listing the universities and colleges within that state. (The tables appear on the CD-ROM attached to the back cover of this report.) Only fully accredited four-year institutions are included, and some institutions are grouped within the system to which they belong rather than being listed separately (for example, San Diego State University is listed as part of the California State University System).

The following paragraphs describe our sources for all the data in the tables.

Universities: The names of each state's universities came from the University of Texas Austin's Web Central, which contains a list of regionally accredited U.S. universities organized by state (Web U.S. Universities, by State, available at http://www.utexas.edu/world/univ/state/).

Federal R&D Funds: All information on federal research and development (R&D) funds is from the RaDiUS (Research and Development in the United States) database (see Appendix A for a description of this database).

Degrees Granted and Public/Private Status: Our first source of information on the degrees an institution grants and whether the institution is a public or private university or college was the U.S. Department of Education, National Center for Education Statistics, Integrated Postsecondary Education Data System (IPEDS) College Opportunities On-Line (COOL) Web site, at http://www.nces.ed.gov/ ipeds/cool/. If IPEDS COOL did not contain this information, we obtained it directly from the Web site of the specific university or college. When IPEDS COOL was not the source of this information, a footnote so indicates and identifies the actual source.

Schools of Veterinary Medicine: Schools awarding the degree of Doctor of Veterinary Medicine (DVM) were identified using the Web site of the Association of American Veterinary Medical Colleges (AAVMC), at http://aavmc.org/schools/schools.htm.

Schools of Medicine, Chiropractic, Optometry, and Pharmacy: We used field-specific Web sites to identify schools awarding the following degrees:

- Medical Doctor (MD). We used the Association of American Medical Colleges (AAMC) Web site, at http://www.aamc.org/members/listings/msalphaae.htm. Please note that all entries specifying "School of Medicine" refer only to the institutions, or portions of institutions, that award the MD degree.

- Doctor of Osteopathic Medicine (DO). We used the American Association of Colleges of Osteopathic Medicine (AACOM) Web site, at http://www.aacom.org/colleges/.

- Doctor of Chiropractic (DC). We used the Association of Chiropractic Colleges Web site, at http://www.chirocolleges.org/collegest.html.

- Doctor of Optometry (optometrist) degree (OPT). We used the Association of Schools and Colleges of Optometry Web site, at http://www.opted.org/about_members.cfm.

- Doctor of Podiatric Medicine (DPM). We used the American Association of Podiatric Medicine Web site, at http://www.aacpm.org/careercenter/cz3_links.asp.

Land-Grant Universities: We used the Cooperative State Research, Education, and Extension Service (CSREES) Web site, at http://www.reeusda.gov/, to identify land-grant universities. This site contains a directory of land-grant universities that are state partners of the CSREES (http://www.reeusda.gov/1700/statepartners/usa.htm). To verify this information, we also consulted the National Association of State Universities and Land-Grant Colleges (NASULGC) Web site, at http://www.nasulgc.org/About_Nasulgc/members_land_grant.htm.

To identify certain historically black land-grant colleges and universities, we used a separate CSREES page, at http://www.reeusda.gov/1890/, which provided information on 1890 Land-Grant Colleges and Universities, and the NASULGC Historically Black Colleges and Universities Web site, at http://www.nasulgc.org/About_Nasulgc/members_HBCU.htm. The 1890 Land-Grant Colleges and Universities are labeled "1890" in this appendix.

Historically Black Colleges and Universities (HBCUs): We identified Historically Black Colleges and Universities (HBCUs) using the 2003 U.S. Department of Education—Accredited Postsecondary Minority Institution Web site, at http://www.ed.gov/offices/OCR/minorityinst.html, and Peterson's Black American Colleges and Universities Web site, at http://www.petersons.com/blackcolleges/bacu_default.asp?sponsor=13.

Student Enrollment: Enrollment data for "All Students," "Undergraduate Students," and "Graduate + First Professional Degree Students" were primarily obtained from the IPEDS "Enrollment at Title IV Participating, Degree-Granting Institutions: United States, Fall 2001" (U.S. Department of Education, National Center for Education Statistics, 2003). When student enrollment data were not available from this IPEDS publication, we sought the information from IPEDS COOL, at http://www.nces.ed.gov/ipeds/cool/. If the data were not available from IPEDS COOL, we went to Peterson's, at http://www.petersons.com, or Hobsons CollegeView, at http://www.collegeview.com. If student enrollment data were not available from either Peterson's or CollegeView, we went to the Web site of the specific university or college and searched for statistics about its student enrollment. If the data were not available on the institution's Web site, we obtained them by calling the university or college directly. Footnotes indicate institutions for which information on student enrollment was not available from the IPEDS "Enrollment at Title IV Participating,

Degree-Granting Institutions: United States, Fall 2001" and provide the exact source of the information.

Note that, in some cases, a school may be accredited to award a master's degree or doctorate, even though no graduate students were enrolled in the graduate program according to the IPEDS "Enrollment at Title IV Participating, Degree-Granting Institutions: United States, Fall 2001." In addition, some schools that offer bachelor's and first professional degrees but no graduate degrees may have a number of students listed under "Graduate + First Professional Degree Students." In this appendix, we have combined graduate degrees with first professional degrees, so the number of students listed under "Graduate + First Professional Degree Students" reflects the number of students enrolled in programs that grant first professional degrees. First professional degrees may be awarded in any of the following ten fields: chiropractic (DC or DCM), osteopathic medicine (DO), dentistry (DDS or DMD), pharmacy (PharmD), law (LLB or JD), podiatry (DPM, DP, or PodD), medicine (MD), theology (MDiv, MHL, BD, or Ordination), optometry (OD), or veterinary medicine (DVM).

Number of Faculty: We obtained the number of faculty at each institution from the IPEDS Peer Analysis System, at http://www.nces.ed.gov/ipedspas/, and the Peterson's Web site, at http://www.petersons.com. When information about number of faculty for an institution was not available on the IPEDS Peer Analysis System or Peterson's, we sought it at Hobsons CollegeView Web site, at http://www.collegeview.com. If information about number of faculty was not available from any of these three sources, we went to the Web site of the specific university or college and searched for statistics about that institution's number of faculty or actually counted the number of individuals on lists of faculty. If the information was not available on the institution's Web site, we obtained it by calling the university or college directly. Institutions for which information on number of faculty was not available from the IPEDS Peer Analysis System or Peterson's are footnoted to indicate the exact source we used. Note that the total number of faculty reported for each institution in this appendix includes both full- and part-time faculty.

Federally Funded Research and Development Center (FFRDC) Operator: Academic institutions that operate FFRDCs were identified using the master list of FFRDCs contained in the National Science Foundation "Federal Funds for Research and Development: Fiscal Years 2000, 2001, 2002" (National Science Foundation, Division of Science Resources Statistics, 2002).

Federal R&D Funds per Capita: We calculated federal R&D funds per capita by dividing the "Federal R&D Funds Received in FY 2002" for each institution by the number of students or faculty at each institution.

Davey, Michael E., and Richard E. Rowberg, *Challenges in Collecting and Reporting Federal Research and Development Data*, Congressional Research Service Report to Congress, January 31, 2000.

Eiseman, Elisa, Kei Koizumi, and Donna Fossum, *Federal Investment in R&D*, MR-1639.0-OSTP, RAND Corporation, Santa Monica, CA, July 2002.

"Federal Procurement Report 2002," available at www.fpdc.gov/fpdc/ FPR2002a.pdf.

Fossum, Donna, Lawrence Painter, Valerie Williams, Allison Yezril, Elaine Newton, and David Trinkle, *Discovery and Innovation: Federal Research and Development Activities in the Fifty States, District of Columbia, and Puerto Rico*, MR-1194-OSTP/NSF, RAND Corporation, Santa Monica, CA, 2000.

Mowery, David, and Nathan Rosenberg, "The U.S. National Innovation System," in Richard R. Nelson, ed., *National Innovation Systems*, Oxford University Press, 1993.

National Science Board, *Federal Research Resources: A Process for Setting Priorities*, National Science Foundation, October 11, 2001.

National Science Foundation, Division of Science Resources Statistics, "Federal Funds for Research and Development: Fiscal Years 2000, 2001, and 2002," NSF 02-321, Arlington, VA, June 2002.

Popper, Steven W., and Caroline S. Wagner, *New Foundations for Growth: The U.S. Innovation System Today and Tomorrow*, RAND Corporation, Santa Monica, CA, 2002.

U.S. Department of Education, National Center for Education Statistics, Integrated Postsecondary Education Data System (IPEDS), collected in Spring 2002 and released in December 2003.

Walshok, Mary L., Edward Furtek, Carolyn W. B. Lee, and Patrick H. Windham, *Building Regional Innovation Capacity: The San Diego Experience*, Industry & Higher Education, Vol. 16, No. 1, February 2002, pp. 27–42.